WISDOM
that leads to
SOUL REST

**TWENTY-THREE PEARLS OF WISDOM
FOR THE DRIVEN OR DRAINED**

Bret Kolman

For other permission requests, contact the publisher at:
Sabbatical Taker, LLC
Bret Kolman
312 SW Greenwich Drive, Suite 785
Lee's Summit, Missouri 64082
Email: contact@sabbaticaltaker.com

ISBNs
Print: 978-1-964677-02-6
eBook: 978-1-964677-03-3
Audiobook: 978-1-964677-04-0

First Edition

Published by Sabbatical Taker, LLC

Cover design by Kayley Kolman
Book design by Publishing Hackers

Table of Contents

Epigraph

Autobiography is only to be trusted when it reveals something disgraceful. A man who gives a good account of himself is probably lying, since any life when viewed from the inside is simply a series of defeats.

—George Orwell

Introduction

IN 2014, I DISCOVERED A rhythm that completely redefined my perspective on work, relationships, and rest. I took a three-day retreat to remote cabins with a friend and spent time in solitude, fasting, brainstorming, reflecting, and praying. It gave me a tremendous boost of energy, creativity, and *soul rest* that a vacation or long weekend never had. It was so powerful that I decided to repeat it at least three times a year, because, paradoxically, pausing wasn't slowing my progress—it was accelerating it.

I got home from my twenty-fifth mini-sabbatical, and I thought, *Wow, these mini-sabbaticals are too powerful to keep a secret. I know so many people who could benefit from an intentional pause.*

I started writing *Wisdom That Leads to Soul Rest* with the idea of sharing why, when, where, and how to take a sabbatical. I went on the back porch and dictated for about four hours. Suddenly, I had the beginnings of almost every chapter, but I realized my career as a hospital CEO was creeping into the book. I couldn't help but add some advice on physical health, leadership principles, relationships, faith, God, and even a chapter on money. It became filled with little nuggets of wisdom I'd picked up along the journey of life, becoming something akin to the Old Farmer's Almanac for the mind, body, and soul.

> This is the book I wish someone had given to young Bret Kolman with a note that said, "Bret, save yourself time, money, and pain. Read this book."

As I experienced *soul rest* over the course of a decade, I realized some of life's greatest lessons defy logic. My wife showed me that losing actually strengthens relationships. Experience taught me that most of my shortcuts turned into longcuts with hidden costs.

I began giving grace freely once I understood it was, by definition, unearned. I watched friends experience their deepest peace in the wake of trauma or a critical diagnosis. I discovered that gratitude is a mindset you can train, even in the hardest seasons, and generosity is an inoculation against greed. This book tells the story of learning those lessons and many more, so you can go further, avoid self-sabotage, and keep from becoming *soulspent*™.

There are lessons for the ultracompetitive, for those seeking a deeper faith walk, or for those who just feel something is amiss. You might be reading this book to reach new heights in your career and grow as a leader, or because recent events have drained your reserves. Either way, *Wisdom That Leads to Soul Rest* is for those who want to lead, love, and live with renewed energy and joy along the way.

You can read this book alone, but you'll find deeper value when you share it with others. When you talk about your journey, you multiply your growth and divide your burdens. If you're willing to be open, you'll find community and encouragement you didn't know you needed. Don't have anyone to read it with? I'll find you someone.

You can contact me at contact@sabbaticaltaker.com.

The journey begins with dirt–and a lesson that reminded me what can happen when we stop working the soil long enough to let God nourish and restore it.

CHAPTER 1

Sabbatical Taker™

Dirt Nap

I'VE ALWAYS BEEN INTRIGUED BY the biblical practice of letting farm-land lie fallow every seventh year. I owned a farm in Kansas, and 2023 marked the seventh consecutive year of my owner-ship, prompting me to think, *Should I let my land go cropless*? When I first mentioned the idea to my wife, she was supportive but nervous.

The farmer with whom I shared crops and expenses found the concept of not planting a crop foreign, if not unwise. "You can't just let the dirt sit there," my farmer advised. "You've got to plant a cover crop to keep the weeds from taking over." Some weeds, once they flower and produce seeds, can remain viable for over seventy years. This advice made sense, and I agreed to plant grass as a cover crop. However, I resolved not to plant anything that would produce income or deplete the soil's nutrients.

What happened to my farm may seem like good luck or a coincidence to some, but I believe it was a God thing. We let the land lie fallow in 2023 and came back with winter wheat that would be ready for harvest in July 2024. There wasn't much rain early in 2024, and crops had a poor start, but I thought, *Maybe I have more moisture in the soil because the grass covered the land.* Not long afterwards, we got much-needed rain, and my soil was ready for it.

As the wheat began to mature, the farmer started sending me pictures and videos of my wheat. He was pretty excited. He sent one photo of the wheat waist high. He was impressed. Then, he pulled a clump of wheat out of the ground, and there were not one but two earthworms working the soil for me.

When harvest time came, my field made double the county average. It was like God made up for the lost year. However, that's not all. The kernels were so perfect they were considered "seed" wheat. Now, any kernel of wheat when planted and watered will grow. Some farmers just use last year's harvest to plant the next year's field, but other farmers buy a larger, more expensive kernel to increase the chance of a bigger crop. The wheat you buy exclusively for planting is called "seed" wheat and costs about twice as much as the wheat you just harvested.

Not only did I have a bountiful harvest that was twice the average, but my wheat was also seed wheat, so it was worth twice as much. That special harvest, blessed by the Lord, was used to plant over 5,000 acres, resulting in another outstanding harvest in 2025.

> This experience reinforced my conviction that rest isn't a wasted opportunity but actually results in unexpected abundance.

Relationships, Emotions, Spirit, and the Body

Wisdom That Leads to Soul Rest will show you how the pattern of the dirt nap has played out over and over again in my life. Sometimes I learned the hard way, and sometimes the smart way–from someone else. I discovered I could be so driven in my career goals, fitness achievements, or relationships that I felt drained. Early on, I thought I could overcome this fatigue with a good nap or a vacation.

Thankfully, about ten years ago, I began to embrace the natural rhythm God built into the universe, which has provided me with deeper rest and more energy. Stay with me on this journey, and you'll discover the secret ingredient most people don't include in their formula for success and drive for accomplishment: *soul rest.*

Rest is counterintuitive and is widely replaced with caffeine, adrenaline, sleep deprivation, and fierce competition. These strategies work in the short term, but over time, they lead to exhaustion, headaches, high blood pressure, adrenalized arguments, and strained relationships. If you stay on this path and ignore these warning signs long enough, you eventually reap a harvest that might include lost motivation, discouragement, broken relationships, self-sabotage, numbness, or depression. I call this little basket of fruit *soulspent,* and it will reduce your capacity to grow and enjoy life.

My goal is to bring all the interconnected areas of *soul rest* together so you can discover simple life hacks that let your natural drive take you further while leaving you **more** rested! Each chapter could fill its own book, but I've brought all these interrelated themes into one place. My hope is that by sharing my lessons, you'll find *soul rest* quicker and counterintuitively go further than continually striving allows.

What's a Sabbatical?

Along the way, I'll introduce the practice of sabbaticals similar to my dirt nap above, but not requiring a year off from work. At its core, a sabbatical is a rhythm of rest, solitude, and silence that interrupts our daily striving, much like the ebb and flow of the ocean. It's about stepping back from the constant drive of life to create space for God to restore your soul. Sabbaticals come in many forms, but I've found four time frames that create a healthy rhythm: daily, weekly, mini-sabbaticals, and long sabbaticals.

A daily sabbatical starts with a good night's rest and a time of quiet for reading, journaling, and praying. It's simple, but not easy, I know. I provide ideas on how to implement this as we go.

A weekly sabbatical is an idea with deep roots in Jewish history. The traditional Jewish day of rest (Shabbat) begins Friday evening and ends twenty-four hours later on Saturday evening. This tradition dates back to the creation story in Genesis, where God created the world in six days and rested on the seventh. An interesting aspect of Shabbat is that it begins at sundown, symbolizing the day of rest starts with sleep, so **even the day of rest begins with rest**.

When I began honoring a weekly Sabbath, I discovered that rest is not a reward for hard work; it is a necessary rhythm for a healthy and fulfilling life. When I was rested, I became more creative, more patient, and more productive. Rest benefited my family, my friends, my work, and myself.

Make It a Mini-Sabbatical

About ten years ago, I discovered a life-changing rhythm of rest that didn't interfere with my job. I started taking three mini-sabbaticals each year with a group of fellow *sabbatical takers*. These begin on Saturday night with a shared meal and end Tuesday morning when we eat "break-fast" and end our sixty-hour fast together. It requires only one workday but allows for sixty hours of fasting, long stretches of solitude, and shorter times of what I call "campfire talk," where you can get wise counsel.

I've completed twenty-nine mini-sabbaticals, some alone, some with my wife, and many with like-minded *sabbatical takers*. While solitude is an essential element of all of them, I've found that doing them with others makes fasting easier and allows me to bounce my ideas off fellow sojourners. It was after my twenty-fifth mini-sabbatical that the inspiration to write this book was born.

Supersize It

Looking back through my mini-sabbatical journals, I first wrote about a year-long sabbatical in 2017: *What's one thing fear is keeping you from doing?* My answer surprised me: *Take a year off from work.*

The idea of taking a year off continued germinating in my mind, but it seemed to be all about land. I was discussing this with my daughter, and I said, "We let the land rest. I guess it's implied that people and animals rest, too?" That's when she said, "What are we made of?" I said, "Dirt!" It felt like a confirmation that a supersized sabbatical was in my future.

That conversation took place in 2023 while the farm was taking a dirt nap, and in 2024, after prayer and wise counsel, I stepped into my own year-long sabbatical. Leaving my role as a hospital CEO wasn't easy, but I sensed God's quiet invitation: *It's there for the taking.* I didn't know what would come next, but I trusted Him to lead me. Halfway through that year, this book was born.

Start How?

Ask God, "What sabbaticals should I add to my life?" Maybe it starts with something simple, like a consistent sleep pattern or a weekly rhythm of rest. Maybe it's gathering a few friends for a sixty-hour mini-sabbatical of fasting, solitude, and campfire talk. Or maybe, in time, you'll sense the call to a longer break lasting months or even a year.

The most important step is to embrace a rhythm of sabbatical rest, even if it costs you time or money. Rest restores, multiplies, and prepares you for what comes next and has the power to expand your capacity and change your life.

CHAPTER 2

Learning to Lose

My wife has given me a lot of relationship advice, and yes, that has multiple meanings. Her advice taught me something about *soul rest* I needed to learn. I call it learning to lose. Some lessons you master easily, but some take a lifetime of practice. You might say learning to lose is my lifetime achievement badge. There has probably been no more important lesson for me.

Growing up, everything was about competition, and sports were my life. I dreamed of playing for the Dallas Cowboys, but fell short of that goal when I maxed out at 5' 10", 150 pounds in high school. Technically, I was on the roster at a higher weight, but I wore ten pounds of ankle weights during my physical. Unfortunately, I was one of those bad winners and bad losers. Don't ask me how long it took me to outgrow this behavior. It was immature and embarrassing.

Susan and I were married in 1991. Early on in marriage, Susan wanted help with the kids and the house. I wanted to spend my time at work and return to school. I somehow thought a verbal disagreement was normal and sometimes entertaining. In my mind, when two people disagree, you make your arguments, and the logical person is the winner. She is more emotional, and I'm more logical, so the deck was somewhat stacked in my favor under these rules, allowing me to win and win and win.

Spousal Jiu-Jitsu

One day, Susan and I were debating, and I mopped the floor with her poor logic. I was winning. That's when Susan hit me with a trick question out of nowhere. She asked, "Do you want to be right, or do you want to be happy?" Full stop. *What just happened? What did you say?* "Do you want to be right, or do you want to be happy?" That's tricky. No one had ever used this logic during a debate. Was that even allowed? I was thinking, *Well, I want to win. Can I take a day to think about it and get back to you?* But thankfully, I didn't say that.

At that time, I was so competitive a part of me wasn't sure which one I wanted more. For the first time, I realized how my drive to win was taking a toll on my marriage, and that got my pea-sized brain thinking about how it might impact other relationships. I might be happier winning in the short run, but I was picking up a hint this might come with a long-term price.

I'm a typical guy, and my emotional intelligence was a little behind the curve. It's kind of funny now, but thank God I listened and learned to stop winning at any price.

That one lesson blessed our marriage and later became integral to my management style and relationship mindset. I stopped debating for sport and trying to always win, and started thinking win/win (gasp, win/lose?).

This was a eureka moment for me when I realized sometimes I would feel like I was losing. This subtle shift in thinking will save you a lot of emotional turmoil, strengthen your relationships, make you more likable, and help you find *soul rest* and peace, rather than competition and pride.

Watch and Learn, Grasshopper

A few years later, my wife took the lesson to another level. I was nitpicking about things like getting places on time, and Susan was nitpicking about things like picking up clothes on the floor. It was the small papercuts of everyday life.

I got this genius idea from a book, the radio, or somewhere. Instead of complaining about minor daily grievances, we should write them down, make a list, and then present it to the other person on Wednesday at 7:00 a.m. We both agreed Wednesday at 7:00 a.m. seemed like the best day and time to dump seven days' worth of complaints on each other.

That week, Susan started complaining about something, and I said, "Stop! Put it on the Wednesday List. It can wait." I felt so good saying that. I laughed the second time I said it. Then she did something that made me want to attack, and she said, "Stop! Put it on the Wednesday List. It can wait."

This went on for six days. I kept track in my head, and I thought, *She might have had more dirt on me than I had on her*, but I didn't write it down. On Wednesday morning, I woke up and rushed around. Crap. I forgot to write out my list, I needed to leave for work, and I literally couldn't remember anything. I saw her note on the table. She had made a list the night before on an 8.5 x 11 piece of paper folded in half. On the outside, the title was "The Wednesday List." On the inside, my infractions?

I opened it. It said, "I love you for providing for this family. I love you for working so hard. I love you for ..."

I read a list of all the reasons my wife loved me, and that was our first, last, and only Wednesday List. Not only was it the last Wednesday List, but the nitpicking seemed to dissolve into thin air at the same time. Yes, I married up!

The beauty of her list was she took a solution that might benefit many marriages and made it exponentially better. Consolidating our complaints wasn't a bad idea. But Susan made a list that would never win an argument, had no logic, and gave me all the power; **she was losing on purpose**. Her letter elevated me rather than dragged me down with my shortcomings. She wrote a letter that took the debate to a spiritual level. It's the most beautifully kind and ingenious lesson I learned about losing.

When I first learned this lesson, I supervised about thirty employees. None of them were physicians, and only a few were leaders of leaders. Later in my career, I was responsible for over 1,500 employees, many of whom were physicians or leaders of leaders.

With experience, I noticed most broken relationships had one person in the relationship who was a winner, like I used to be. They unconsciously pushed and pursued victory so hard they ignored the relationship costs.

I remember working with one particular physician who had a history of broken relationships. He came into my office to discuss an issue, and it was like a perfectly crafted legal argument, complete with supporting documents. He wasn't wrong, but we could have addressed his concerns three months earlier on multiple occasions; however, he wanted to ensure he won. He wanted to be the smartest person in the room.

That's when I shared my wife's advice and added my own summary I had coined. Susan's advice was, "Do you want to be right, or do you want to be happy?" Bret's application is,

> "If you win every debate, you lose every relationship."

I went to school for many years to obtain fancy degrees and credentials, but my wife taught me a life hack you don't learn in a classroom.

Sometimes in relationships, we feel like we are compromising or even losing. By all means, always strive for a win-win outcome. I'm not suggesting there needs to be a loser. Just know, sometimes your emotions may lead you to believe you are losing, and that may be precisely what is necessary for the sake of the relationship.

People Business

Part of having strong relationships, whether with coworkers or spouses, is appreciating and respecting what others bring to the discussion. Every person has unique experiences, knowledge, talents, and abilities. They bring all those personal traits to the table when making a decision. You can show how much you respect and appreciate their opinion and unique characteristics by giving them a substantial voice.

Employees and co-workers feel they have a substantial voice when they are listened to, and their ideas are included in the solution. For the ultracompetitive person, you may sometimes feel like you're losing on purpose. It's okay. In fact, it may be the humility your employees need to see in their leader.

This is a crucial lesson because we are all in the people business. Therefore, relationships are the key to enjoying life and big accomplishments. You may not think you're in the people business, but if you work with a boss, a customer, or a coworker, or even live with or socialize with another human being, you are in the people business. If you are accomplishing big things, you are undoubtedly working with people.

Would you like to have better relationships? Let other people win. Let someone else's idea be the winning idea. You will develop those around you and have stronger relationships.

Losing doesn't mean compromising your morals or your standards. It doesn't mean running meetings like a democracy where everyone gets an equal vote. It doesn't mean announcing, "I am going to let you guys have your way." It means some issues aren't worth debating, and some battles aren't worth winning.

If you have an ultracompetitive personality, you might be inclined to "win at all costs." However, those costs often include strained relationships, sleepless nights, ruminating thoughts, and adrenaline-fueled arguments.

Winning is great. Win/win is even better. If you're someone who can't bear to let others win, you'll find yourself caught in an energy-draining and relationship-damaging cycle. If you work or live with this person, make a copy of this chapter and give it to them. Learning to lose on purpose and choosing your battles wisely might be the energy hack you need to find *soul rest*. Those around you will benefit, and ultimately, so will you.

CHAPTER 3

The Gift of Grace

THOSE WHO'VE WORKED WITH ME know I've always been big on grace—probably because I need more than most. That's why I developed a saying I often shared with my team during the years I was learning the *sabbatical taker* lifestyle:

> "Give the grace you want."

- Would you like a lot of grace? Then give a lot of grace.
- Would you like to be judged by your intentions rather than your actions? No worries; do the same for others.
- Would you like to be able to explain yourself fully before passing judgment? That's a good idea. You should listen fully before you pass judgment.
- Don't like it when people categorize and label you based on one or two data points (maybe your worst moments)? Then don't be so quick to categorize and label others.
- Does someone in your life like to remind you of past wrongs? Don't remind them of past wrongs.

- Do you want others to speak highly of you? Then speak highly of others.

It's not complicated. When you want something, be the first one to give it. It may not be fair or reciprocated. That's okay. Do it anyway.

A Business Is Born and Dies in 90 Days

Early in our marriage, Susan and I invested in a business with some sweet people. I wish this were the story of how we all became billionaires in my garage. It is not. We wanted to sell large and small satellite TV receivers. It looked like the future, as customers finally had alternatives to cable. I never dreamed I would eventually be able to watch TV on my phone.

We placed an ad in a local newspaper (it was a long time ago) and received an immediate response, resulting in a large sale with a nearly 300 percent profit. Based on our huge sample size of one and our eagerness to make it big as quickly as possible, we did not seek additional counsel. Instead, we jumped in whole hog by investing all of our free cash, and my partner quit his full-time job to work the business.

For about thirty days, it looked like a good idea. Around day thirty-one, we got our first cash call—if you're not familiar with this term, don't become familiar. Susan went to the bank and got a cash advance on our credit card. It seemed logical at the time, and we had already invested all our cash. I think our little venture lasted a little over ninety days before it blew up.

Not only did the business blow up, but so did the friendship. I wrote a nasty letter demanding my money back. It was not my finest moment. My partner and his family moved, and we lost touch. It's a sad reminder that often the fantasy of getting rich and friendships don't mix.

I thought at the time, *Maybe I should take them to court and get a judgment.*

Right, Rights, and Grace

I knew if I took them to court, a judge would see it my way, right!?! I wanted to assert my rights and ensure everything was fair, but the Lord dealt with me and told me to forgive it and give grace instead.

It hurt because it was a lot of money at the time. However, in retrospect, it was my fault, too. It took me at least ten years to see how my overconfidence, not counting all the costs, and not seeking other wise counsel, played a role in the business failing. I don't know where they are today, but I pray they are blessed.

Picking up your rights and enforcing them will cost you time, money, sleepless nights, and peace, among other tolls. It's not a free transaction. The tax keeps accumulating like interest; plus, we may not even like the decision of a third party. Serious crimes deserve justice, but even then, we will have to forgive if we want *soul rest.*

However, most infractions are minor, such as people disappointing us or not taking ownership. Then, we hold on to those offenses, and those people begin to occupy space in our heads without paying rent.

Releasing your rights is one of the most energy-freeing choices you can make because enforcing them will inevitably disrupt your *soul rest.* Doing so will enable you to move forward without dwelling on past hurts. You will soon sleep better and be able to use your time and talents to develop your future dream or vision.

Stable Relationships

Grace is most needed for those we are around often. That's because relationships are messy. There's a great proverb that says where there is no ox, the stable stays clean, but if you want a big harvest, you need an ox. I once cleaned a horse stable that had about four inches of mess. It wasn't fun.

What is the point of this proverb? It's not just about oxen. It's about people, too. People will make a mess in your stable, but you won't have a big harvest without other people.

No employees? Great, no staffing problems. No friends? Great, no time wasted hanging out. But would you like your life to be bigger than a party of one? Then you'll need people; inevitably, people will make a mess in your stable. And, don't miss this: You will make a mess in their stable, too.

> Relationships require grace because they are inherently messy.

All this messiness requires grace. That's why I also say, **"Grace is the lubricant of relationships."** If properly cared for, your car may go 300,000 miles, but it won't make it 5,000 miles without oil. That's because oil lubricates the engine. Relationships aren't easy, and they become even harder when you don't give grace, leading to more friction and increased tension.

Grace at Work

Grace makes the workplace far more enjoyable. We likely spend as much time with our co-workers as we do with our family. Sometimes stakes are high and relationships can be strained. There's a good verse that says, "If possible, so far as it depends on you, be at peace with all people."[1] Be a peacemaker at work.

I'm not suggesting allowing incompetence. There's plenty of room for grace without allowing incompetence. However, relationships built under the strain of position, money, or power are likely to have a limited shelf life, with no printed expiration date. Inevitably, employees leave to find a workplace built on influence, respect, and grace. These are sustainable ways to build a relationship.

If you are part of an interview process, I encourage you to hire people who share your attitude toward grace, as it can impact workplace culture. Here's a hiring question that helps find employees with a high emotional quotient (EQ) and who likely offer grace:

> "What misperception do people have of you?"

I love this question because there is no such thing as a misperception. People's perception is their reality. How an applicant answers tells me a lot about their overall EQ and social awareness subcategory. Introspective people are aware of their weaknesses and are working on them, so they feel more authentic and approachable, and are better judges of when to hold someone accountable or give grace. If you hire introspective people, they will be harder on themselves than you ever could—so give them grace.

Grace at Home

Family is the group of people who prove love covers a multitude of sins. I'm sure they would say the same thing about us. Living under the same roof as another human being takes grace. We have to look past numerous imperfections and show love with our words and actions. If you are experiencing difficulties in your marriage because of a grace disparity, get counseling. A third party can provide tips and tricks they've learned from their education and experience.

Parenting is challenging because we are transitioning from using force, if necessary, to a coaching approach. As our kids mature, we have to pivot from using our power to persuasion, teaching them to evaluate situations and make good decisions. Eventually, we are left on the sidelines as coaches, using loving influence and giving the grace we would want to receive. Sometimes, we forget we weren't perfect kids either. It begs the question: Would you like to be parented by someone like yourself? Find the delicate balance between grace and consequences through prayer and love.

A Harvest of Grace

There's a principle at work in nature called the law of the harvest. When you plant corn, you get corn (same). You plant one seed, but harvest many seeds (more). The corn takes about four months to grow (later). The law of the harvest is (1) same, (2) more, and (3) later, and this law doesn't just work for corn; it works for generosity, kindness, and, importantly, for grace, too.

You may be scared to give grace. You may fear being taken advantage of, or you give it begrudgingly because you never received it. There's a great story in the Bible where people are encouraged to "give and it will be given to you pressed down, shaken together, and running over."[2] This entire story is about the standard we use to judge others—i.e., do we judge harshly or give grace? The message of this story is give grace and you will receive a harvest of grace pressed down, shaken together, and running over. You will reap your biggest harvest after you've sown it repeatedly, accumulating a reserve for when you need it most.

If you live a life without giving grace, it will wear you out. You will experience a hole in your energy bucket and a lack of *soul rest* due to the increased friction in your relationships.

CHAPTER 4

Learn to Love the Word "No"

THE WORD THAT WILL TUCKER you out more than any other is "yes." That's why there is so much power in the word "no." This simple word controls our calendar, our health, our finances, our relationships, and even our emotions. You can't say yes to every meeting, all the snacks, every purchase, or 1,000 intimate friendships.

It's a "No" for Me

If you are good at what you do, like to serve, or have many giftings, everyone will want a piece of you. There are only so many pieces of you to give in twenty-four hours. The valley between the current you and the rested you may be filled with a bunch of opportunities you need to say no to.

- Would you like to order out? No, let's eat in as a family and save money.
- Would you like to join our club? I'd love to, but I won't be able to make the meeting and give 100%. You guys deserve better.

- Would you like dessert? No, my doctor said I have to watch my blood sugar.
- Would you like one more time with your addiction? No, I promised my accountability partner I wouldn't. I want to be a person who keeps my word, and they said they would check in with me every week. I don't want to be a liar.
- My poor planning has created a crisis in my life. Can you help me dig out of it? Wow, that sounds horrible! I know how you feel—I feel overwhelmed, too. It's like God gives us all we can handle in twenty-four hours. Unfortunately, I can't help you without creating a bigger crisis in my own life. I'm so sorry. How about I cook extra tomorrow and bring you guys a fresh meal instead?
- Would you like to buy a new car? I sure would, but the one I have right now gets me from point A to point B, and I decided to stop trying to impress everyone.

> Oh my gosh, with two no's you can change your week, and with five no's you can change your life.

Are your yeses overcommitting you and stopping you from enjoying *soul rest*? No can be your new favorite word!

The professional askers and those close to us know how to turn up the heat with short timelines, guilt, and appeals to our pride. Those emotions don't help us, so don't make decisions when you feel pressured, helpless, or when there is an appeal to your ego. Stop and ask for more time.

When someone says, "But sir, the discount is only good for the next thirty seconds, one hour, or three days," I say, "Okay,

I was leaning toward 'yes,' but you made my decision easy. I won't be rushed into a decision. No, and goodbye!"

Have there been times you said yes and later wished you had said no?

> There is so much power in saying no because you can always go back on a no. It's hard to go back on a yes.

Here's a little list to remind you. What would you add?

The power of saying no is you can:

- Control your calendar so you aren't overcommitting and ensure time for critical priorities, such as family or sabbaticals.
- Keep you from overspending.
- Control your tongue so you don't say things you regret.
- Control your fleshly appetites so you don't fall victim to physical addictions.
- Control your diet and exercise routines.
- Keep you from trading the temporary for the eternal.
- Keep you focused on long-term benefits rather than short-term desires.

Emotionally Attached to Yes

On the other side of the equation are the times when people tell us no. I don't know about you, but life would be so much easier if I got everything I asked for. I don't like being told no! As a matter of fact, I've discovered I don't always handle it well.

For much of my life, I've had a bad relationship with the word no ranging from disappointment to frustration. Sometimes we can have an internal dialogue with ourselves when we are told no, such as: "They (God or people) don't want the best for me." Or, "I failed." Or, "They're not rejecting my idea, they're rejecting me." We can create untrue narratives when we hear this one simple word.

Early in life, I discovered a common workaround to being told no that saved me a lot of frustration. I stopped asking for permission and asked for forgiveness instead. How clever was I?

This little shortcut ended up costing me a lot of time, money, and pain, and I learned I wasn't much different than Adam and Eve in the garden. Adam was given a clear directive by the Lord not to eat the fruit in the middle of the garden, or he would die. It was a hard, non-negotiable no. One day, a deceiver came along and appealed to the **lust of the flesh, the lust of the eyes, and the pride of life**. These are the same motivators causing problems today.

The deceiver entered the garden, questioning what God really said and suggesting that God was holding out on them.

"When the woman saw that the tree was **good for food**, and that it was a **delight to the eyes**, and that the tree was **desirable to make one wise**, she took some of its fruit and ate; and she also gave some to her husband with her, and he ate."[3] In that moment, their eyes were opened, but instead of gaining freedom, they felt shame and tried to cover themselves.

At the heart of the conversation is the implication that God doesn't have your best interests at heart, which leads to questioning and not fully trusting His no's. Once they stopped trusting, they found a way to justify their actions, thus asking for forgiveness instead of permission. As a result, it cost them peace and resulted in a fallen world for all of us when they rebelled against God's no.

Wait, didn't God say they would die? We are, of course, physical and spiritual beings, which is why we need more than a long nap to recover from being *soulspent*. Their spirit died that day–more details at www.sabbaticaltaker.com.

Sometimes, no is protecting you from something in your job or family and is providing rest for your next season. No may keep you from being fired, or, counterintuitively, it may protect you from a promotion you or your family can't handle currently. In your marriage, it may be protecting you from a divorce, dividing your assets in half, and juggling your kids 50/50.

When you trust God, you trust His no's. Usually, His no's come through those in authority over us. Trust Him in those times and pray for those in authority over you.

In the workplace, no's can provide inspiration for a better sales pitch. Recently, I was working on a group project when we heard the dreaded "no." My emotional response kicked in, but instead of getting frustrated, I wrote this list to reframe my thoughts when I heard no. I sent this as an email to everyone.

The benefits of being told no:

- When told "no," you will gather more information to improve your pitch.
- When told "no," you will seek additional advice and explore alternative solutions.
- When told "no," you will generally look for a cheaper and easier way.

- When told "no," you will find out what your absolute must-haves are.
- When told "no," you will discover new timelines.
- When told "no," you will look for more scripture and pray more.

Start reframing your "no's" as a gift by believing you can trust God and those in authority over you. Maybe it's a temporary no and really just a request for more information. Go get that yes—after you ask God if you have the right motives!

Bottom Line

How you handle the word no is at the epicenter of your success, failure, and fatigue. First, stop dreading saying no to people. Don't let people pressure you into saying yes.

Likewise, if you don't like hearing no, maybe you have an old no wound from feeling controlled. Ask God to check your motives, and if all clear, present a better case!

The word no is powerful and can refresh your soul. Learn to love it, use it, and respond to it properly.

CHAPTER 5

I Have One Word for You—Submit

DURING ONE OF MY SIXTY-HOUR mini-sabbaticals, I was challenged to choose a word for the year. This word would lead, guide, inspire, and instruct me for the next twelve months. I closed my eyes, expecting a great revelation, and said a little prayer. The word "submit" came to mind. Why did I think of that? I don't even like that word. It tastes like egg whites, and I was thinking of something more chocolaty, like "blessings" or "winning."

I tested the word in a sentence. "Lord, I submit my _____ to you." I tried filling in the blank. I submit my career. I submit my marriage. I submit my kids, finances, desires, life, or anything else I could fill in the blank. I tried the word in another sentence: "Help me to obey, respect, and submit to _____." I thought of some people I could fill in the blank with, and it hurt a little even thinking about it.

I felt trapped when I heard the word "submit" because I knew exactly why God was giving me that word. It was almost as if He was trading on insider information. I already had a good working knowledge of submitting, but God wanted me to pursue a PhD.

Over the next twelve months, God gently sanded away imperfections by reminding me to submit to specific situations, people, and organizations. I didn't want to be sanded. I was pretty happy with my imperfections. They were easy to explain and often justified with, "That's just how I am." Who can argue with that logic?

The truth is, the sentence goes more like this, "Yes, I know that's how I am...I probably should change...But I don't want to change." You have to get to the point where you value the future version of yourself so much you are willing to go through the pain of change.

Sometimes, God asks us to do something for our benefit, but it may be a little painful. It's like explaining to our kids the dentist will hurt momentarily, but the relief will last a lifetime.

Beginning with that sabbatical and throughout the rest of the year, I started to see how often my prayers revolved around getting my way. I wanted outcomes to work out the way I thought they should because, of course, I knew best. When the results didn't work out according to my plans, I became frustrated. As I began submitting more, my perspective shifted. I started thinking about submitting in every area of my life. I began to trust that decisions made by others would ultimately benefit me.

You're Only Hurting Yourself

Once, I was obsessed with a building project that kept getting denied due to cost constraints. I couldn't get it approved, even though I was pushing with all my might, doing my research, praying, and making a better pitch. It was driving me crazy and giving me a bad attitude. It wasn't good for my mental health or career.

Then, one day, I came across this line: "It is hard for you to kick against the goads."⁴ It was such an odd sentence. I looked it up and realized it was meant for me in that season. You see, goads were sharp sticks at the front of an ox cart meant to teach a stubborn ox that kicking only hurts itself. That was me: kicking, fighting, and bruising myself against something I couldn't change.

This sentence was God's way of saying, "Stop kicking!" I let go and found peace rather than a new building. If I had received approval for the building, I doubt I would have applied for my next job, where I learned about mini-sabbaticals. I got a promotion instead of getting fired. That was many years ago, and I still think that building was a great idea, but God had something even better for me. Trust Him.

Are you injuring yourself by kicking the cart? Do you have trouble submitting in general? Your frustration may come from the government, the IRS, a spouse, a teacher, a coach, a parent, or a boss.

I like to say, "If you don't like gravity, create your own universe." Don't complain about the rules and laws, but do nothing. Choose to stay and submit or leave and create a better version of what's frustrating you. But leaving is easy. Typically, leaving just means finding the same frustrating people and situations with new names and new locations. I suggest you stay and work on changing yourself instead by learning to submit.

Our first test in submission comes from our parents. I believe God sent us a clue about submission by where He placed obedience to parents in the Ten Commandments.

The first four commandments focus on our duty to God and are vertical–like earth to heaven. They include commands like loving the Lord and not using His name in vain. After that, the commandments address our interactions with others—don't lie, don't steal, and so on. These are in a horizontal orientation because they relate to those around us. The fifth commandment, about honoring our parents, is squeezed between the four vertical commandments and the five horizontal commandments.[5]

God shows us He puts us under authority, and we are to honor and obey our parents "in the Lord," meaning not matters that are illegal or immoral.[6] Our parents are both an authority (vertical) and a relationship (horizontal). They represent a bridge between God as an authority over us and the rest of the world.

Rebellion

Let's look at the word submit from another angle. What's the opposite of submit? I think the opposite is to rebel. Were you rebellious as a youth? Maybe you'd like to call it something nicer, like "stubborn" or "long-suffering." Perseverance is no doubt a Godly trait in the right context–when it is rooted in God's will. However, when long-suffering is rooted in self-will, it is a type of rebellion.

When I was young, I was rebellious toward coaches when we were losing. It was a trait God had to work out of me. Have you been rebellious, stubborn, and selfish toward your spouse instead of preferring the other person? Which attitude will fill up your energy bucket faster and stop the daily energy leak— submission or rebellion?

Have you ever considered actions or decisions made ten or more years ago and realized you acted out of rebellion? That rebellion comes with an emotion, or perhaps we should call it a spirit—a rebellious spirit. Acts and words of rebellion are fueled by anger, bitterness, jealousy, and maybe, just maybe, looking back ten plus years, you realize wrong motives, too.

The spirit of rebellion is dark and evil and does not come from God. Rebellion will steal your peace, keep you at odds with others, leave you feeling fatigued, and leave you distant from God. That's why submitting is so vital to finding *soul rest*.

It's believed Satan was an angel who rebelled and took other angels with him. He's the first rebel, and he wants us to join him. He offers lies and half-truths to convince us. His ways lead to destruction and pain. Without submission, we reap more of Satan's counterfeit peace and economy.

Submitting to the Outcome and the Process

In this journey of submission, I have to say, "Not my will, but Your will be done."[7] It may not be easy, and we may feel like we are being asked to give up our dreams or goals.

Ask God in that time of frustration, "God, what are you trying to show me? What are you saving me from? What better thing do you have for me?" One verse says, "Humble yourselves in the presence of the Lord, and He will exalt you."[8] The greatest show of strength is to lay down our desires and our will and trust in a higher plan. Of course, I'm not talking about submitting in illegal, immoral, or unethical areas.

Submitting to the outcome includes submitting to the process. We are happy to submit to the process of eating a steak. We don't want to skip to the end when it goes down the sewer system. But when life is frustrating, we start looking for shortcuts. We want to walk through our new building without resubmitting our proposal over and over, or sleep in our new home without experiencing contractor delays.

The process is where we develop discipline and character. The process is lifting weights every other day for three months and eventually celebrating a healthier, fitter you.

Skipping the process means going to bed one night overweight and out of shape and waking up the next day able to bench press twice as much and losing twenty pounds. Skipping the process is cheating and steals the growth and joy of developing the mental discipline to wake up and work out. Do you want the outcome so badly you will cheat to get to the end?

Skipping progress can have serious consequences if you have a family-owned business. You may want your kids to step in and run the large company you built, but if they don't work to develop their business and emotional intelligence, they may wreck it. They have to go through the process, the ups and downs, the missteps, the problem-solving, and learn the business from the inside out. We can't save our kids from the process, and God doesn't save us. Instead, He is using the process to develop us.

There is joy in the journey if you embrace struggle as part of the process and decide in advance to find joy in all circumstances. Then, you will look back on your life and realize the process is what made you who you are today, and you will be able to encourage your kids or others when their process becomes messy.

Somewhere along the path, submitting will undoubtedly be a lesson to learn and a struggle to grow from, just as showing love to the unlovable, forgiving those who hurt you, or showing patience are.

> Don't wish the hard times away, and as a result, wish life-changing moments away.

Instead, lean in and engage in the process. It gradually changes us as we submit the outcome and the process to the Lord. We begin to find joy and rest even in difficult journeys.

Don't rebel against the outcome, don't skip the middleman, and don't skip the process. Instead, choose to submit because rebellion could be what's keeping you from enjoying *soul rest*.

CHAPTER 6

Feedback Loop of Life

IN LATE 2025, MY MOTHER-IN-LAW gave Susan and me a love note she stumbled across while going through old keepsakes. It was from 1991 in my handwriting, but I had totally forgotten I had written it or what I said. The three of us opened it and read together as I declared my undying devotion. It was sappy, nerdy, and embarrassing to read in front of my mother-in-law. Apparently, at that time, I thought it was best to explain our love in mathematical terms. It was sort of this formula that explained the odds of meeting such a wonderful person. You may ask what exactly it says, and I will gladly post it for $1 million.

As if page one wasn't humiliating enough, there was a second page where I apologized for being sarcastic and promised to do better. Uh oh, there it was—my little feedback loop of sarcasm—still alive and active thirty-four years later. By this time, we were all three laughing, and I was hoping I hadn't promised to give her a foot massage every night, too.

Apparently, after I turned 180 degrees away from sarcasm in 1991, I just kept turning in a perfect circle like a lighthouse, over and over again, during the days, months, and years that followed. I've received intense spousal coaching on this through-out the decades.

Your cycle may be different, but your pattern is likely the same: You have a bad habit that hurts you or others, it causes pain, you apologize and stop for a season, but later go back to your bad habit. How many times you go around and around is up to you. Some people never get off the merry-go-round.

Pain is Feedback

Part of seeing and identifying the cycles in your life is noticing why pain exists and how you cope with it. God gives us pain as a natural form of feedback. I get drunk; I feel sick. I stop for a while. I get drunk; I get in a fight. I stop for a while. Hmmm. I wonder if there is a pattern with drinking too much. What about other patterns like anger, worry, or overspending?

It's hard to deal with the feedback loop of life when we continue to ignore, mask, hide, numb, and bury our pain. There are healthy and unhealthy ways of dealing with pain. One brings rest, while the other brings weariness and counterfeit peace, counterfeit joy, counterfeit love, etc.

You may feel the price of paying attention to the feedback provided by pain is costly, but ignoring it costs even more. When we ignore or excuse our behavior away, those bad habits take root and grow in size and impact and steal our *soul rest*. That's why finding our patterns and embracing authenticity matters.

Emotional Nuance

Once you start paying attention to your pain, think about the emotion you feel right before you go for another spin on your favorite ride—maybe it is rooted in fear, anger, shame, or pride. But let's try to be more nuanced in discovering our emotions. Below is a table that reads from left to right, starting with fruit, then branches, and ending with roots.

I have named this table The Thorn Bush in honor of its behavior in nature. The thorn bush produces small, bitter fruit that is not good for eating and often can make you sick. Its branches are brittle and filled with sharp daggers that dig into the flesh of any who dares come near. It has small leaves that provide almost no shade. Its roots are aggressive and sprawling; they are built for survival, not stability or strength. The roots send out suckers, helping it form a colony that doubles every eighteen months. Its roots dominate the first eight inches of soil, allowing it to horde water and choke out other beneficial plants. It doesn't need good soil because it can live in soil that is rocky and uncared for. This little bush represents our bad habits—the destructive feedback loop of life. Our good habits are represented by the olive tree and can be found at my website: www.sabbaticaltaker.com.

Let's do a little soul-searching to identify this nasty habit of sarcasm I have. I looked at the thorn bush of emotions to see what I was feeling when I was sarcastic. I see my sarcasm best described as the fruit of **frustration**, from a branch supported by **blocked desire**, nourished by the roots of **anger**. Ouch! I don't like my sarcasm when I see it described this way.

The Thorn Bush of Emotions

THE FRUIT How We Feel the Emotion	THE BRANCHES Why It Forms	THE ROOT Emotion
Resentment, Outrage, Bitterness	Injustice	Anger
Frustration, Irritation, Impatience	**Blocked Desire**	**Anger**
Defensiveness, Distrust	Violation of Boundaries	Anger
Anxiety, Worry, Insecurity	Threat of Loss	Fear
Panic, Helplessness, Avoidance	Loss of Control	Fear
Envy, Suspicion, Inferiority	Jealousy (Nested)	Fear
Arrogance, Defensiveness	Insecurity	Pride
Contempt, Dismissiveness, Bitterness	Desire for Superiority	Pride
Perfectionism, Inflexibility	Fear of Weakness	Pride
Humiliation, Self-Loathing, Isolation	Self-Rejection	Shame
Embarrassment, Inadequacy, Insecurity	Fear of Judgment	Shame
Sadness, Despair, Helplessness	Unresolved Grief	Shame

Note: You'll notice that some of the fruit, such as helplessness, can appear in multiple branches because it can grow from different roots.

Internal Audit Department

During the last ten years, while I was finding *soul rest* through purposeful pauses, mini-sabbaticals, and later, my one-year sabbatical, I stopped ignoring pain. Instead, I asked what it was trying to teach me. Recently, I've become more nuanced in how I describe my emotions so I can better label the feelings that lead to my sarcasm or bad habits. Next, I decided it was time to call in the dreaded internal audit department.

Our minds are working in our subconscious behind the scenes. I would say it always works for our good, but that isn't true. The subconscious world works for our pleasure, preservation, and safety. My physical body is concerned with me, myself, and I. The problem is most of these subconscious desires conflict with our long-term best interests. Only with God's help can we rewire our subconscious to stop it from maintaining a loop that focuses on short-term "me, me, me."

That's because God's plan is for our long-term benefit, requiring us to submit, prefer, and serve others. When we choose the short-term over the long-term, we will end up with cuts and bruises that will result in pain, scars, and trauma. We can't change the past, but darn it, we can stop doing the same painful things in the future...with God's help.

I try to intercept my subconscious thoughts with a simple internal audit question: "What am I thinking, and why?" The more you do this, the more you realize your mind is listening to the same news feeds, radio stations, TV channels, and advisors with the same information day after day.

We are tuning into the person, church, or school of thought that broadcasts the message we prefer to hear. Psychologists call this confirmation bias. It means we have a subconscious bias to ignore or not listen to people who think differently from us.

It could be that your confirmation bias is keeping you from changing the channel you are listening to or breaking off an unhealthy relationship. You may need to break the pre-cycle first. This, in turn, will change your thoughts and emotions, which will change your behavior and stop the negative feedback loop in its tracks.

> The feedback loop of life looks for patterns in the stations you listen to, the friends you choose, the resulting emotions you feel, the actions you take, and the words you speak.

Hearing Aids

When I go on a mini-sabbatical, I try not to do all the talking. I'm listening for God, too. The Bible describes God's voice as a gentle whisper. If your radio station is tuned in to the loud voices of TV, social media, worry, and adrenaline, you may not be able to hear the gentle whisper. As a matter of fact, you must listen intently. That's why times of silence and solitude are so important to hearing that quiet voice. Then, once you start tuning into the right station, you might realize the feedback loop of life is causing pain, and that pain is trying to point you in a different direction.

It will be hard if you haven't practiced listening. Many times, you have practiced the counterfeit by surrounding yourself with noise and activity. By practicing quiet and stillness, you will find God is speaking. You will learn to tune in to God's radio station with practice and discipline.

> God describes it this way: "Pay close attention to what you hear. The closer you listen, the more understanding you will be given—and you will receive even more."[9]

If you listen carefully, you will hear, "I love you. Go and sin no more."[10] When we recognize the feedback life is giving us, we stop the vicious cycles of addiction and pain. Our souls find rest as we label our emotions and audit our thoughts while listening to God's gentle, loving whisper.

An easy way to start is to turn off the noise of social media and your phone before bed so you can sit in silence and reflect on the day. Even better, you might want to start your morning with quiet time to set the tone for the day ahead. With God's help and discipline, we experience *soul rest* when we break harmful habits.

CHAPTER 7

Storm and Scars

On August 23, 2005, the National Hurricane Center (NHC) identified a Tropical Depression off the Bahamas coast. The next day, the winds reached 40 mph, and the storm intensified to a tropical storm. By August 28, Hurricane Katrina had strengthened to a Category Five hurricane with peak sustained winds of 175 mph. It slammed into the coasts of Louisiana and Mississippi, dropping up to twelve inches of rain in twenty-four hours with a peak of three inches per hour.

Even though everyone saw it coming and tried to be prepared, unless you live in a bomb shelter, you cannot prepare for 175 mph sustained winds and twelve inches of rain. It was brutal. An old boss of mine slept in a flooded hospital for four days before he was evacuated by helicopter.

My friend Glenn, whom I met around the time I started mini-sabbaticals, lost everything during that storm. He was married with three kids under the age of thirteen. Talk about a gut punch and a scary time.

He and his wife decided to take a drive and try to figure out what to do next. They left their home at 1:00 p.m., headed south, and about that same time, forty-five miles away, a truck towing a boat left the south shore headed north across Lake Pontchartrain. While crossing the US Highway 11 Bridge, the boat came off the tow hitch, crossing multiple lanes of traffic and slamming into their car, killing his wife. If it had been fifteen seconds earlier or later, the boat would have missed them altogether—one stoplight or one more trip to the bathroom.

I won't try to explain this situation away as a good thing. This was a painful and traumatizing event that left a mark on Louisiana, countless families, and especially on Glenn and his family. If you've ever had surgery, you know scars leave a mark that tells a story about your life. Some scars are unseen, left on the heart, the soul, or the mind, and tell stories most people don't know about us. What do your unseen scars reveal about you, and how long did they take to heal? Finding healthy ways to deal with wounds so scars heal makes finding *soul rest* easier.

Like a hurricane, you may not have had control over your storm, but perhaps it was a series of poor judgments, and even now, you struggle to forgive yourself for bringing on the storm. God is a merciful judge, so throw yourself at the mercy of the court and ask for forgiveness. God can make a way where there seems to be no way.

Sometimes, we struggle with the age-old question: "Why do bad things happen to good people?" There's a saying, "He causes His sun to rise on the evil and the good, and sends rain on the righteous and the unrighteous."[11] The reality is storms will come into our lives and the lives of those we love. It's not a matter of "if," but a matter of "when." The question is, "What will you do when storms hit?" Will you let the storms of life define you or refine you?

As we process life's storms and life's trauma, we might be tempted to let a traumatic event define us. No doubt, an event like losing your spouse will change your life, but it doesn't have to be an anchoring event that holds you in place and stunts your growth. We can respond in faith and still find *soul rest* even in the storms of life.

When I've talked with people who have experienced the horror of cancer, hurricanes, and other storms, I've found surprising grace and peace from those who found a healthy way to heal. God provides grace specific to each person's storm, and others around them are not given the same measure of grace. The grace is specific to the person and their storm. God puts ointment on the one who is wounded. Greater need equals greater grace.

Foxglove Leaves

This principle is even evident in nature. The leaves of the foxglove contain cardiac glycosides, and only two or three leaves can be fatal. Physicians discovered in the 1800s that small doses could be used to treat "dropsy," or what we now call congestive heart failure. Today, there are over one million doses of digoxin given under numerous brand names from those same poisonous leaves, but in a much smaller dose. This drug strengthens the heart's contraction and slows it down, making it more efficient. As a result, patients shed the excess fluid and find relief from shortness of breath.

God knows your diagnosis and has the exact dose to bring you healing.

> God can use the poisonous events in your life to bring healing to you.

Later, God may use you to be the carrier of the healing dose to someone else caught in the same trauma you once were.

20/20 Vision

You might look back and realize the storm was the only way God could get your attention because of pride, arrogance, or greed. The biggest takeaway for cancer survivors in a 2023 survey was "I see what is really important in my life" (Yao et al. 2023). This is not an advertisement for a better and happier life through cancer. There are costs, inconveniences, and pain in our storms, but somehow, studies show God brings a supernatural measure of grace and peace, helping us see life differently after the storm. God's grace gives us the faith to believe that He is working in all things to bring about a positive outcome for His glory.

Dig into your situation and ask God to help you, be with you, and strengthen you. He will, and He does. Avoid the temptation to blame and accuse God for storms and trauma. Talking with God about our feelings and asking hard questions is good and natural. I think there is a time when these honest questions seeking to understand can cross over and become angry, ruminating accusations that God isn't who He says He is. That angry, recurring thinking will stop you from finding *soul rest*.

Prescription

While you're digging through the rubble of your storms, look for specific scriptures that are just the right medicine, such as "I know the plans I have for you. Plans to bless you and not to harm you" or "Cast all your cares on Him because He cares for you."[12] Let God apply medicine, so the root of bitterness doesn't start growing in your life.

The lesson I learned from Glenn is to praise Him in the storm. It's the opposite of being angry and will lead to your wound healing. Being angry at God is like rubbing dirt on a wound. It won't heal if you keep touching it with dirty fingers of accusation.

Mad, For You

There's another important lesson in trauma and storms: Don't become offended for someone else's hurt. Picking up someone else's offense and becoming angry and bitter is not the best way to help a friend. In anger, you might give bad advice, or the root of bitterness may grow in your life, poisoning your relationship with yourself, others, and God. It will steal *soul rest*. The wounded person receives a different measure of grace than the observer.

That doesn't mean we don't help our wounded friends by praying with them and encouraging them. You may be God's hands in action. God doesn't order from Uber Eats, so He might use you to start a meal train. Your challenge is to serve and empathize without getting sucked into their pain so deeply you become angry and bitter.

As God works in and through the person who is wounded, the storms and trauma they went through becomes their testimony, and they can use it to help others. Alternatively, they can miss that testimony and never let it develop because they choose to hold a grudge or be angry. Those emotions indicate that healing is still needed physically, mentally, or emotionally. Our assignment is to avoid anger and resentment from our trauma, and to avoid picking up someone else's pain and becoming angry on their behalf.

Wanna Trade?

When I'm on sabbatical, I share my concerns with others, and at the end of the discussion, I'm remarkably content to take my problems home. I don't want other people's problems. I'm not equipped because the grace was given to them, not me. I've been surprised to learn the same is true in discussing challenges with other organizational leaders around the conference table. I learn from them, but I don't want their problems.

The longer I've walked with God, the more I trust Him. As my faith grows, I've become increasingly confident the **storms of life are happening for me, not to me**. It's a mindset rooted in faith. Over time, I have seen how God is faithful in my life, and when you surround yourself with the right people, you hear how He is faithful in their lives, too.

Science confirms we become like those with whom we spend time. According to a 2021 NIH study, "The Power of Peers: Who Influences Your Health," birds of a feather do indeed flock together. Surround yourself with strong relationships that will help you learn to operate in faith. You'll stop wishing you had someone else's life. Plus, they will be the ones to start the meal train, pray with you, and be there for you after the storm passes. The right friends will provide words that become a healing balm to your soul. Find those people.

My friend Glenn is one of those people, and hearing his testimony strengthens my faith. He's remarried to a wonderful, godly woman. Life has changed a lot; as it has, he's chosen to be filled with faith, joy, and praise. He has a ton of energy and is fun to be around. That's what proper healing looks like. Other people without his faith give in to alcoholism, depression, or worse. Not Glenn; he's an inspiration.

Fleece Fatigue

I want to challenge you in your faith because faith is a decision, yet faith can't be proven. There's an interesting story in the Bible about a gentleman named Gideon. His job was to fight alongside 299 others against 135,000 enemy soldiers. This is the kind of job you don't volunteer for; instead, you are called to it. In his case, people were selected based on how they drank water.

Gideon was a little nervous and wanted a miraculous sign. He left a fleece lying on the ground overnight. He prayed, "Lord, if I'm being called, give me a sign. Make the fleece wet and the ground dry." And in the morning, it was so. The second night, he wanted a second sign. He prayed, "Lord, if I'm being called, give me a sign. Make the fleece dry and the ground wet." And in the morning, it was so.[13]

With these two signs, Gideon had enough proof, enough confidence, and enough faith to obey God's call. I have a question: How often will you ask for a "fleece" or a "sign"? Is two enough? Or is it 100? Do you trust God in the storms? Do you have the faith to obey when it doesn't make sense?

As your faith grows, you will ask for fewer fleeces. As your faith grows, you will trust He is working all circumstances for your good, even when it doesn't make sense. As your faith grows, you will come to believe nothing happens to you that is not happening for your greater good. And as your faith grows, you will find peace in the storms and a deeper sense of *soul rest*.

CHAPTER 8

The Faith Journey of Parenting

I WANT TO ADDRESS THE faith elephant in the room—our children. How many of you can raise your hand and agree when I say, "Kids are the gift that keeps on giving"? Our kids bring us immense ongoing joy, but they can also be a source of frustration.

We often feel pressure and guilt, thinking, "Good parents always have good kids who behave perfectly all the time." That notion only holds up in the armchair world, where we dispense advice to others about raising their children.

Somewhere around my seventeenth mini-sabbatical, I was sitting around a campfire with many people I knew well. At this point, we had already been doing mini-sabbaticals together for years and sharing our deepest concerns. It wasn't until years of sabbaticals, prayer, and solitude that I came to appreciate just how universal the burden of young kids, teenage kids, and adult kids was.

Parenting is a hidden world most don't openly discuss, and it can quietly drain our emotional energy, becoming a major barrier to finding *soul rest*. As our kids grow older, we start to miss the days when the most significant "problem" was convincing them to eat their vegetables.

A six-year-old child might ask, "How did that baby get in your tummy?" or "Why is Dad living somewhere else?" We will answer them in language a six-year-old can understand. Then, we turn around and ask God, "Why did you let Hurricane Katrina destroy my house?" It's complicated, and we may not fully understand or accept the answers we receive. Our children give us a small glimpse into the relationship between our Father God and His children...us. As our kids grow older, our concerns deepen to dating, drugs, alcohol, mental health, driving, friend groups, social media, and so on. It's hard to know just how insulated from the real world we should keep them.

Every challenge your child faces is an opportunity for them to grow in their faith—and for you in yours! Faith is like a muscle; the more you experience trials, the stronger your faith gets. We want big stories about how God came through for our kids, but an easy life for them (and us). We don't want hardships. That's why the Bible says, "Consider it nothing but joy, my brothers and sisters, whenever you fall into various trials."[14]

I think most of us would rather suffer than see our kids suffer. We want to save them from their mistakes, natural consequences, financial hardships, and other adverse outcomes. The hard times shape who we are, but we don't want our kids to experience any hardship. Nature gives us an example of this. Farm-raised fish never tastes as good as wild-caught fish. There's something about the dangerous life of a wild fish that leaves it tasting better. Those wild fish are searching for food instead of being fed. There is something about struggling that is good for them.

Least Happy Dominator

There's a mentality that's easy to adopt, but one we must resist: "We can only be as happy as our least happy child." You may have subconsciously adopted your child's level of happiness. For example, if my oldest child is going through troubles and is crying every night, I might feel depressed, too. It's a natural instinct, but it's also a trap. There's a danger in letting our children, spouse, or circumstances control our emotions. We can't give in to these thoughts; it will drain us. We will not only become *soulspent*, but every other area of our life will suffer as well because we become exhausted, depressed, anxious, and overwhelmed.

Let me give an example from one of my mini-sabbaticals. My friend Darren went on his first mini-sabbatical with us in 2018. Darren is a one-of-a-kind, incredibly gifted guy. His son Cameron was born with Hypoplastic Left Heart Syndrome (HLHS), which means he was born with half a heart. As a result, doctors said his lifespan would be shorter on average.

I can only imagine the strain on him and his wife when they got this news. We can all agree this is stressful and could steal our joy. But bad news, bad circumstances, bad luck, and other stressors don't have to steal our joy—not if we don't let them. Joy is not the same as happiness. We can have joy in all circumstances because joy is internal and part of the fruit of the Spirit. On the other hand, our external environment and emotions influence happiness.

Darren found people of faith to pray with him about Cameron, to pray specific prayers and give glory to God for who He is, not just for what He does. Prayer can move God's hand to change His mind.

There are at least six instances recorded when God changed His mind. The most well-known is probably Jonah and Nineveh. Another example is Hezekiah being given fifteen more years of life. In Darren's case, he moved the hand of God because Cameron is now twenty-one years old and doing way better than projected. He's a calendar savant and has written an entire fantasy series.

You might struggle with this theology because "none of your prayers have been answered." First, that's not true. God answers all prayers. Sometimes, the answer is "no" or "not right now." Sorry, there's no guarantee that you will get a "yes," or that God's plans will change.

Sometimes, the most important part of prayer is drawing closer to God, not the specific answers. His ways are higher than ours, and He is sovereign, so He doesn't have to explain Himself.

> However, there is a 100% chance that joining others to pray and seek the Lord will change you.

Plus, it will put you in the right friend group with faith-filled people.

We pray for the best, but God walks with us if it turns out to be the worst. Not getting what you want in prayer can make some people angry, and they declare themselves enemies of God. They call Him names, avoid a relationship with Him, and attack people who seek Him. I promise this will drain your energy, steal your *soul rest*, and prevent you from showing your kids how to have joy in all circumstances.

If that's not enough, you will teach your kids to let their anger energize and fuel them, to count on no one, to trust no one, and to look out for number one. Observe the Feedback Loop of Life in families who use this teaching model and see how it works. Instead, let us show them our faith because we know they will have many troubles in this world, but **fear not**—God will go with them through those trials and tribulations.

I want to encourage you because I know God has and wants you to experience *soul rest*, and it will also be a gift you pass down to your kids. It's a vital anchor we give our kids when we teach them to find peace during life's storms. They are developing their faith with our help. We can remind them God loves them and has their best interests in mind, and we should trust Him, not blame Him. Teach them to ask, "What can I learn from this?" instead of "Why me?" They learn "how to learn" versus becoming a victim.

I Saw Midnight

I want to leave you with an assignment. This is an idea of how to pray for your kids that my sabbatical brother taught me. It's a one-time, three-week commitment. The twenty-one-day commitment is based on an Old Testament story in Daniel, where Daniel had committed to pray. He didn't hear anything for twenty-one days. After twenty-one days, Michael the archangel showed up and said, "I left heaven to come to you when you started praying, but there was a delay in the spirit realm that kept me from arriving." If you want something big for your kids, you need to pray when you aren't seeing or hearing a peep.[15]

This assignment invites you to surrender your children to God, entrusting Him to nurture their faith and guide them through life's challenges. It's built on the mnemonic "SPIRIT."

- The S stands for "Spiritual"—pray, and that they develop a deep hunger for God, directed toward His truth.
- The P stands for "Physical"—ask for their health and safety under His care.
- The I stands for "Intellectual"—seek wisdom from the Lord for their decisions and circumstances.
- The R stands for "Relational"—pray for strong, godly connections with friends, family, the Lord, and authorities.
- The second I stands for "Income"—ask that they're blessed with resources to bless others.
- The T stands for "Talents"—pray they discover and refine their gifts for God's kingdom.

I've added an online form for the twenty-one-day challenge, available at www.sabbaticaltaker.com.

The twenty-one-day challenge involves setting your alarm to wake up at midnight and pray for your kids for one hour, Monday through Saturday. On Sunday, let your corporate worship be your time of prayer. Paul and Silas had a breakthrough at midnight, so there is power in the supernatural at midnight, which can be for good or bad—make it for good.

Each night, you pray on just one letter from the mnemonic "SPIRIT," and repeat the process each week for a total of three weeks. It doesn't matter if you have one child or ten. The idea is you are disciplining your body and intentionally coming before God while they are sleeping and dreaming, calling on God to move in their lives. You are giving it twenty-one days, so there will be breakthrough in the supernatural realm. The sacrifice you make of your regular sleep schedule is like the sacrifice of food during fasting. God sees our sacrifice and honors our extra effort.

I did the twenty-one-day challenge after my friend shared this idea with me. If you love your sleep as much as I do, you know this was a sacrifice. As with all matters of faith, I can't prove it helped, but I believe it did. Even if the exercise didn't change my kids, it did me. Once you've gotten out of bed at midnight for three straight weeks, you will find more *soul rest* because you gave your burden (your kids) to God. In addition, your spiritual muscles get bigger when you move in obedience, faith, and discipline. Spiritual exercise will increase your hunger and appetite for spiritual bread. The twenty-one-day challenge was a one-time assignment that permanently increased my ability to pray longer. Give it a try.

CHAPTER 9

Gratitude

I'VE LEARNED I DON'T HAVE very good manners. Often, I forget to say, "Thank you," especially to God for all His blessings. When you need an answer to a prayer, feel worried, or find yourself in a foxhole, you cry out for help with weeping and often lose sleep. When your prayer is answered, you stop crying and sleep like a baby. We put a lot of energy into "Can you help me?" "Please," and "I need it," etc. But we often don't have much energy left for "Thank you."

Sometimes, the burdens we pray about drain our energy the most. Worry, disappointment, and grief are slow, constant drains on our energy bank. We have to fight back against these energy leeches with gratitude. Then we need to access the faith region that trusts that everything is working for our benefit and fills us with hope for a surprise ending we will love.

Life Fell Short of Expectations

I want to compare the journey of life with a bike ride I've done across Iowa called RAGBRAI. It's a 500-mile bike ride over seven days, come rain or shine. The year I turned forty, I signed up to challenge myself and to prove my youth, even though it would cost me a week of vacation. I was joined by over 8,000 participants. It was so exciting and exhilarating to see different bikes and interesting people all in one place the night before the start.

During my training, I had been busy and had only gotten up to riding 100 miles in a week. I was nervous that I wasn't prepared, but I didn't want to back out on my two friends, who were both older than I was and hadn't trained much more. I figured I could just slow down if worse came to worse. On the first day, I started a little tired, since I wasn't used to sleeping in a tent, showering from a hose, or waiting in a porta-potty line to go to the bathroom. But once I got on the road, I was rolling!

I had a nice road bike that kept my head down for aerodynamics, and a little 3x5" seat, so I didn't add too much weight to my bike. My shorts had built-in cushioning, and the weather was fantastic.

Have you ever seen those memes with a picture of someone, and the caption says, "How it started," and the next picture's caption says, "How it's going"? Yeah, well, that cushion in my shorts and that little 3x5" seat turned hateful after about 250 miles, and I found out about a little thing called the pudendal nerve. In addition, my hands were numb from leaning forward to keep my head down into 25 MPH winds and scorching heat.

I used a service to transport my luggage and set up a tent to sleep in each night as I rode from town to town. Apparently, they'd seen this movie before, because they had a sign that read:

"If you're not having fun, lower your expectations."

My expectations were dancing the limbo when I rolled into the last town. I think it took two weeks to recover from that "vacation."

The truth is, disappointment is the gap between what we hoped for and what we received. Often, it is this gap that can rob our spirit of joy. That saying cracks me up, and I still mention it when someone says they aren't having fun.

Sometimes life hands you more than a vacation gone awry. Perhaps you've been marinating in disappointment for so long you've become discouraged and lost hope. Faith is the substance of things hoped for and the evidence of things yet unseen. When you lose hope, you begin living a life of fear, doubt, and discouragement.

To protect your emotions, you become Eeyore from *Winnie the Pooh*. By expecting the worst, you're never disappointed. You're already on defense, putting up a wall to guard you from more emotional and psychological damage, leaving you bricked in and unable to be open to nurturing from gratitude, faith, and hope.

Gratitude Gardening

Feelings of gratitude can be cultivated. Gather people around you so the input you are receiving is positive. Anchor yourself in positive messages like this: "Let us not grow weary or become discouraged in doing good, for at the proper time we will reap, if we do not give in."[16] Take time to renew your spirit and ask God to show you reasons to be grateful. Consider consulting with a wise third party, such as a professional, who can provide unbiased advice.

We all face times in life when our expectations don't match our actual experience. After five years of college, I still hadn't met my wife, like a lot of my friends had. The longer I went alone, the more disappointed and discouraged I became. There was work God was doing in me before I could meet Mrs. Wonderful. I had to practice my faith walk to grow my faith muscle.

One Sunday, I decided visiting one church a week was too slow, so I called around to churches and asked about their services. I called a particular church, and my father-in-law-to-be, who was a greeter, answered the phone and persuaded me to come. I met my wife, and fifteen months later, we were married.

I worked hard to find my spouse. People who know us both say she's a saint, and I'm a saint-maker. I prayed a lot. I worried I might never find a wife, but even now, I don't always do a great job of showing my gratitude for having a great spouse. I don't naturally say "thank you" to God. I don't say "thank you" to her. I've learned I must practice gratitude intentionally if I want it to be a habit.

Gratitude List

An attitude of gratitude is the perfume around our neck, and those who come within smelling (smiling) distance will sense it. If you struggle to be grateful, you give off a negative vibe. Yes, a lack of gratitude is something people can see and feel. Perhaps you are angry, hurt, or resentful about how life has turned out. You have to exercise your gratitude muscle. There is research galore on this topic that shows after just one week of keeping a gratitude journal, you will see the world differently. The science is fascinating, so I included three studies in the references.

Why does this work so consistently? The psychology behind it is a combination of attention bias (Kahneman 1973) and the frequency illusion (Begg et al. 1986). The more common term is Red Car Theory (Clear 2018).

How this works isn't complicated, so let's look at an example. You drive to work each day, thinking, seeing, feeling, and experiencing millions of things, yet you only absorb a fraction of them. One Monday morning, you proudly drive to work in your new red Ford F-150. Suddenly, there are Ford F-150s everywhere, and the car next to you is an ugly red compared to yours, and you wish the trim on your red truck matched the trim on the pizza box. You see F-150s and red everywhere you look. That's the frequency illusion and your attention bias at work, looking for what's important to you.

When you start a daily gratitude journal, your subconscious says, "I'm going to have to remember ten good things tonight. I'd better look for something to be grateful for right now." You are tricking—no training—your mind to pay attention to the good, so you have no brain power left to pay attention to the bad.

Paul encourages us this way: "And now, dear brothers and sisters, one final thing. Fix your thoughts on what is true, honorable, right, pure, lovely, and admirable. Think about things that are excellent and worthy of praise."[17] Wow! Sounds like Paul was encouraging us to be grateful, knowing it would impact our entire viewpoint.

You might be thinking, "Yes, but this isn't real. My life sucks. I'm just brainwashing myself." Well, for starters, your brain needs a good "warshing" occasionally. It regularly fills up with fear, uncertainty, and doubt (FUD) with little effort on your part. You have to intentionally choose to see the other side of the coin.

It's All Good

Jocko Willink, a former Navy SEAL, created a three-minute YouTube video titled "GOOD." I encourage you to listen to it. One of his subordinates always brought him problems, and no matter the problem, his response was always the same: "Good." Here are a couple of quotes from this video: "We didn't get the new high-speed gear? Good. Keep it simple." "Didn't get the new promotion? Good. More time to get better." Every "bad" thing has a "good" thing embedded in it.

No matter how thin you make the pancake batter, there are always two sides to the pancake. One side is disappointment in the outcome, and the other side is the "good" we find in it anyway. Exercising your gratitude muscle will make it grow, and the trials that make your life seem difficult can be reframed in a more positive light.

Like Jocko, who found "good" while fighting life-and-death battles, you can train yourself to look for it and say it. Or, like Paul, who was beaten, shipwrecked, and imprisoned, you can find joy in every circumstance.

Prayer Journal

I've also come to realize that it's hard to be grateful for blessings we can't remember. My brain plays in the short-term memory arena. I have an excellent memory for things I must handle in the next few days or weeks. But ask me about a vacation from five years ago, and I can't remember the names of all the towns we visited, the hotels we stayed at, or any other details.

I often forget all the prayers God has answered, so I learned a trick from a doctor at work. He told me, "The shortest pencil is better than the longest memory." When I was young, my dad was the guy with five pens (all different colors) and a pocket protector. Of course, each generation must be cooler than the previous one, so I use a smartphone instead of paper and pen. I use it for journaling. I don't enjoy journaling, but I've found I need and benefit from it. I have chosen to do something hard to get the benefit.

We are warned, "Here on earth, you will have many trials and sorrows. But take heart because I have overcome the world." In another place, it says, "Be thankful in all circumstances."[18] Life won't always be fun or easy. When you are deep in prayer and come through those difficult circumstances on the other side, a proper response is, "Thank you." Maybe it becomes a habit with practice.

The more you know, the more you are aware of the vibes you give off. You won't be tempted to blame your boss, spouse, kids, job, finances, or anything else out of your control. The struggle is real...but God helps!

Gratitude is your best medicine against the diseases of anxiety, resentment, forgotten hope, and entitlement. When you count your blessings, it refreshes the weary soul. An attitude of gratitude is a sign of a rested soul because gratitude and dissatisfaction can't coexist. Eventually, gratitude pushes those damaging lies out because it says, "No, I've got a lot to be thankful for. I can trust the Provider to provide again." As a result, gratitude refreshes the soul.

CHAPTER 10

Overcoming the Scarcity Mentality

THERE IS A PATTERN OF thought that impacts your health and mindset, known as a scarcity mentality. It's closely related to worry and rooted in fear, anxiety, and distrust that you won't have "enough." The truth is, most people don't feel safe until they have fifty years or more of "enough" stored away.

Each Thanksgiving, my aunt brings a magical chocolate chip cookie. She swears she follows the package recipe, but no one has ever been able to duplicate them. People will grab five or six about an hour before lunch and hide them so they don't miss out. There has never been a leftover cookie at Thanksgiving. It's never gotten carving knife crazy, but it's a battle for a precious resource with a limited supply, so it becomes competitive. If you eat a cookie, someone didn't get one.

Our minds are built to fear the loss of precious, limited resources, such as chocolate chip cookies. It's natural and happens constantly in different areas of our lives. Job promotion at work? If I don't get the promotion, someone else will. Twenty people are being laid off at the factory? If I don't keep my job, someone else will get it. Is the nonprofit asking for a $100 donation? If I give, I'll be left without coffee this month.

The key to scarcity is fear, and fear-based thinking is a cancer. In my twenty-nine years in management, I've never seen a good manager lead by fear, nor a bad manager lead by faith. The managers people least want to work with or for are fear-based. They are scared of working short, getting fired, having people quit, being disliked, being blamed, having their staff outperform them, having their staff promoted away from them, and more.

As a result, they can't lead authentically because they never want to appear flawed or admit that they might not be perfect; therefore, employees don't want to work for them. People can sniff out fear a mile away. Perhaps you've worked for someone like this or have led in this manner yourself.

Fight or Flight

The scarcity mentality doesn't trust God and says, "I won't have enough. God doesn't have a good plan for me. He has rejected, forgotten, or doesn't love me." These are all terrible ideas that are "scare-city" thoughts.

This mindset triggers the amygdala, which activates our fight-or-flight response; as a result, chemicals such as adrenaline, noradrenaline, and cortisol are released into our bodies. (See references at the end of the book to gain more understanding.) These stress-related chemicals increase our blood pressure and alertness, allowing us to think more quickly, run faster, jump farther, and escape danger.

These chemicals are so powerful they need to be used sparingly in a natural ebb and flow; otherwise, they can make you sick because your heart is constantly beating a little faster, your blood pressure is a little higher, and your senses are on high alert.

A few years ago, my wife was out of town, and I was at the neighbor's house watching football until around 10:30 p.m., so I was the only person there. I came home, and the door was unlocked since I was so close by. I fell asleep and woke up around 2:00 a.m. to go to the bathroom.

I checked to make sure the front door was locked and thought I saw a shadow move along the upstairs wall. My heart began to race, and everything loose got tight. I wondered if someone had snuck in while I was next door. I stood listening as quiet as a field mouse.

I've played many games of hide-and-seek outdoors, and motion and sound give you away. I thought about calling 911, but decided it might be premature since I hadn't seen any more motion. I made a stealthy mad dash to grab my phone next to the bed and return to my lookout station next to the stairs. My plan was to make a run for the front door if I saw someone on the walkway heading toward me.

Luckily, one of my sabbatical brothers lived across the street. At 2:00 a.m., in a hushed voice, I called and asked him to come over. I greeted him at the door in my underwear. I now held a steak knife. He had a bat. He could tell I was scared and ready to fight or outrun him. In the back of my head was my mom's voice warning me, *"Don't run with a knife in your hand."*

We quietly crept upstairs and explored every nook and cranny. There was no one and nothing. Apparently, it was my overactive, scared-of-the-dark imagination.

Next time I think there is a murderer in my house, I will probably die rather than have my friend laugh himself to tears telling others about showing up at my house with me in my underwear holding a steak knife.

The point is you don't have to be in actual danger to activate your fight-or-flight system. You just have to think you are in danger. Your scarcity mentality may be keeping your imagination busy. You may be creating frightening scenarios like losing your job, your kids getting in an accident, flunking an exam, going bankrupt, and every other fear you can dream up. Could we train our imaginations to use this power for good instead of evil, like we did with gratitude? Hint: yes. (See references at the end of the book.)

The scarcity mentality puts your imagination to work when it should be relaxing. It's a significant factor in why you need *soul rest*, sabbaticals, and intentional pauses to embrace the natural ebb and flow that includes peace and stillness; otherwise, you become *soulspent*. When you are driven to keep going without purposeful pauses, your body will send you signals like headaches, lack of sleep, illness, discouragement, and even depression. These are the symptoms that often send us to our healthcare provider.

Emotions Versus Logic

Your amygdala has a lot of power because it sits basically in the middle of your brain and gets the first shot at your thoughts before they make it to the logic center at the front of your brain. It can hijack your thoughts, influence your emotions, send you into a fit of rage, or tie your stomach in knots before logic even has a chance to weigh in, causing you to make quick decisions and speak words you later regret, rather than thoughtful, prayerful decisions run past wise counsel. Sometimes, you must give your thoughts time to outmaneuver your emotions.

The older I get, the more I realize not all decisions or debates have to be settled immediately. When I sense emotions are getting high, I look for ways to de-escalate the conversation or take a break from the meeting. The vast majority of timelines are self-imposed or more flexible than initially thought.

Chris Voss talks about how it's true even in hostage negotiations in his book *Never Split the Difference.* Don't let your emotions hijack the meeting or undermine wise judgment.

The challenge is to start ferreting out this inclination toward scarcity, distrust, worry, and anxiety. These are all fear-based emotions, and you may not even realize your subconscious imagination is the triggering mechanism. The problem is, the more often you have these ideas, whether it be consciously or subconsciously, the wider and wider the road in your brain becomes.

We refer to these mental pathways as habits, and they enable us to be more efficient. It's like putting on your seatbelt for the 10,000th time. You don't even think about it. If you're in the habit of thinking or worrying about having enough, your fight-or-flight response will kick in without you even realizing you activated it.

The Cure

How do you get rid of scarcity, worry, and other fears? The same power to imagine fearful situations can be used to imagine a wonderful future, especially if we can believe in faith God loves us, because perfect love will push out fear. When you reach a point where you understand the Maker of the universe loves you, then you know He has your best interests at heart, and He's going to work things out for your long-term benefit. You may not see it, but you choose to believe it before the proof shows up.

You stop blaming circumstances and being a victim and start celebrating circumstances and being a victor. You get to the point where you say, "I don't understand it, but I trust anyway." This combination of choosing to believe in God who loves you and knowing He is working the details out for your benefit is the secret sauce to overcoming fear and scarcity.

Give your secret sauce some meat and potatoes by memorizing some truths you can dig into when ugly thoughts come. Here are a few:

- "For the Lord your God is living among you. He is a mighty savior. He will take delight in you with gladness. **With his love, he will calm all your fears**. He will rejoice over you with joyful songs."[19]
- "**How precious are your thoughts about me, O God**? They cannot be numbered. I can't even count them; they outnumber the grains of sand. And when I wake up, you are still with me."[20]
- "Such love has no fear because **perfect love expels all fear**. If we are afraid, it is for fear of punishment, and this shows we have not fully experienced His perfect love."[21]

Is there anything wrong with believing God loves you and has your best interests in mind? I don't think there is, but you are the boss of you. Free will is a beautiful thing.

Putting It All Together

So, working backward, we have a loving God who casts out all fear and has our best interests at heart. We start to grow in a thing called "faith," which we might have abandoned due to past data points. When thoughts hit our amygdala, we can ignore them or tell them where to go so that our emotions no longer control us.

As a result, fear pathways begin to shrink, and subconscious beliefs are addressed logically and prayerfully rather than emotionally. Our bodies are less tense and more relaxed because they aren't awash in stress chemicals, so we sleep better and feel better. We start finding more joy in the journey, and don't get anxious or angry as easily.

We see the silver lining in all the clouds because we trust there's a surprise ending we will love. We look for the other side of the pancake and say "good." We incorporate intentional pauses as periodic resets that help us align with our natural ebb and flow, thereby leaving us feeling refreshed and providing new perspectives. Wow, sounds good to me. Where do I sign up?

Letting Go Brings Rest

You can't hold onto a scarcity mindset and find *soul rest* because around every corner, there will be a feeling the other shoe is going to drop, bad news is around the corner, or it's all temporary. Let it go by choosing to use your brain's power to remember love, joy, and peace instead of fear, doubt, and anxiety.

CHAPTER 11

Good Decisions

MAKING THE RIGHT DECISION CAN save a lot of pain and suffering. I've made some bad decisions and had regrets. Looking back, there were common attributes in these bad decisions: pressure to make a quick decision, going against my initial intuition, a desire to make someone else happy, dissenting opinions, and lingering doubts.

Sometimes we make a decision before we have an answer from God. My sister wanted to start a clothing line in Thailand—a place she had visited often. She met a nice lady from Canada at an industry conference who had all the answers and plans to launch her product.

She prayed about it but didn't get an answer. She took silence as a "yes" and proceeded. That woman stole all her clothes, and many months later, she had to go to Canada to retrieve them at the police station. No answer isn't a yes; it's a wait.

Lastly, you might make a decision that turns out differently from what you expected. Jesus went to a mountain and prayed all night before selecting the twelve disciples. In that group of twelve was Judas Iscariot, who, over the course of time, became a traitor.[22]

I don't think Jesus made a bad decision or was surprised by the outcome. He did everything flawlessly, but the end result is kind of surprising to us, given who the decision-maker was. Your decision-making process may be perfect, but that doesn't mean things will work out as you expect. People or circumstances might change over time, or God may take you on an unexpected path.

The Four-Step Plan

There are four steps I always take before making a big decision. I might not get it right, but I want to reduce the risk of errors and minimize the cost.

- Run it past wise counsel: "Without consultation, plans are frustrated, But with many counselors they succeed."[23] I don't make life-altering decisions alone in a vacuum, and neither should you. Be sure to share all the facts with your trusted advisor, not just the ones that will lead them to agree with the decision you've already made. A life lived with openness leads to fewer and smaller mistakes.

  How do you choose a wise counselor? Look at their track record. The past is the best predictor of the future. Choose wise counselors who share your worldview. This is more than making sure they have the same political affiliation as you. Do they have the same view of God and His Word that you have?

- Ask God for His opinion: "But if any of you lacks wisdom, let him ask of God, who gives to all generously and without reproach, and it will be given to him."[24]

You can pray, journal, and see what comes to mind. He might have already provided the answer in His Word if you do a little research. I often like to pray, "bless or block." This means if it's meant to be a yes, help it to go smoothly with lots of blessings and open doors. If it's meant to be a no, then shut doors and create barriers. This isn't foolproof. I heard a billionaire speak, and he said he had the ability to open closed doors. You may have the resources to open closed doors, too. A prayer and an open door can't be the sole decision-making tool to guide your life or your family's life when the stakes are high. God gives us wisdom, and part of that is following a process.

- Test it with your peace. There's a story in the Bible about the disciples going out in pairs. They were told if their peace goes out and sticks stay at that place, but if it returns to them, then leave that place.[25]

  Peace is a secret weapon in our arsenal of decision-making and part of walking in the Spirit. Sabbaticals enable us to unplug and experience true peace. You have to experience authentic peace to have something to compare it to.

  Bank tellers don't research counterfeit money; instead, they spend lots of time with real money. Then, they immediately recognize a fake. It's the same with peace. Spend time experiencing it so you know when it's missing.

  This is a good verse that reminds us that peace is a fruit and gift of God's Spirit: "For the kingdom of God is not eating and drinking, but righteousness and peace and joy in the Holy Spirit."[26]

My mom always said, "If in doubt, don't." If you aren't sure you feel at peace, then don't proceed.

- Go on a sabbatical. Since I always have a mini-sabbatical planned right around the corner, I don't make decisions with long-term ramifications or over a certain financial threshold without first going on a sabbatical.

Following wise counsel, prayer, Spirit-led peace, and waiting for a mini-sabbatical provides a solid foundation for decision-making. Time is on your side. Don't give up your advantage by rushing. Sometimes, God is testing your patience and trust, or with time, the original facts start to wobble.

Avoid Big Mistakes

I don't know if you can ever be 100% right in all your decisions, but some mistakes are more costly than others. Sometimes being right will impact the rest of your life.

There's probably nothing more impactful on your life here on earth than who you marry. If you marry the wrong person, that will likely be the gift that keeps on giving. I told my son if he wanted to be a millionaire, start with five million dollars and get divorced twice. He would be a millionaire, if he were lucky.

I see people getting married later and later in life, and I think part of it is the fear of making a mistake. If you've had broken relationships in the past, you start second-guessing yourself and wondering if you have a broken picker. In self-defense, you don't decide. You live in limbo for eight years, dating, living together, and being unofficially married. I've heard this described as getting the milk without buying the cow.

Later in life, you may be deciding where to live, work, or invest your money. All of these decisions are stressful because the stakes are high. There are common ways we escape the weight of the decision. For example, randomly decide with the flip of a coin, so it isn't really your decision. Alternatively, you may never decide, which is the equivalent of a slow no. I hate a slow no. Just say it: "no." Yet another way is to let everyone else decide for you, so you are swept along for the ride.

The problem with this style of decision-making is that other people's priorities define your life, and likely won't be a life lived on purpose. Instead, it's a life lived by accident. I doubt you will find sabbatical rest stops and generous giving along an unplanned route.

Some decisions seem obvious, but without the proper values, people struggle. Do I want to melt heroin in a spoon, draw it into a needle, stick it in my arm so I can feel good for a while? I think I'll pass. I met someone online, and they want to get drunk and have sex. No thanks! Where do your values come from? I align my values with God's Word since it is filled with everyday wisdom.

Follow the Plan

Despite all this good advice, I still don't bat 100%. I've found the best plans are almost always unanimous, but agreement doesn't guarantee the right decision either.

Once, I invested in a company. It had employees and was a small investment. I ran my decision by my trusted advisors, my wife, and prayed, bless or block. There was even a mini-sab-batical before my money was due. I didn't have any concerns and had peace about it.

However, about thirty days before my check was due, I got a promotion at work that caused me to relocate. I really hated to go back on my word and didn't see why it made any real difference. As I got closer to moving, I wanted that cash for a down payment on a house. Plus, as D-Day grew closer, I uncovered a few new "facts." This is unbelievably common in business deals because the devil really is in the details of the transaction. I began to have reservations.

However, I didn't want to be embarrassed by changing my mind. It's the same silly reason that keeps me from doing in-store returns. It's not logical. That uneasy feeling of doubt was a warning sign. I went through with that investment, and what I received in return was a total loss and a tax write-off. Grrr.

It's great to have a solid decision-making process in place. The last step is to follow it. Don't be a victim of guilt, ego, pride, or embarrassment. Don't stay in a place, a relationship, or a business deal when your peace leaves. Cut your losses. Take pennies on the dollar. Don't stick around to find out how the story ends. Get wise counsel so you can do it ethically and legally, but skedaddle.

When you make decisions from peace and *soul rest*, you avoid the toxic motivations of fear, pressure, anxiety, and what-ifs. You avoid mistakes that cost you time and money, leaving you more to give your family, friends, and faith.

CHAPTER 12

Find a Trusted Advisor

Do you have a friend, spouse, or trusted advisor who can offer you brutally honest feedback? If the answer to that question is "no," you might be isolating yourself or getting defensive when people try to share their point of view. When you block feedback, you are doing it for ego or self-protection, but it takes a lot of energy and resources to be your own soul protector and leads to feeling *soulspent*.

Early in my career, I hired a great doctor fresh out of residency. He was great at his job, and we enjoyed working together. Then, because of a series of small misunderstandings and spurred on by a pot stirrer, he decided the town was bad, the job was bad, and I was a horrible person. I don't even remember the details, but I remember thinking it was a molehill that turned into a mountain. He resigned and wrote a scathing letter, which I wish I had kept. I was telling someone how crazy his accusations were. That person said, "He's probably not 100% wrong. You should see what you can learn from it."

It was great advice that made me look at every person's feedback in a different light going forward. I share this story to say: Don't worry if you don't have a trusted advisor; the world will provide competitors, angry customers, angry employees, authority figures, or even enemies to tell you the criticisms you don't want to hear. In fact, they may not even say them to your face, but share them out of context and twist them for everyone who will listen. I doubt they are 100% right, but they're rarely 100% wrong, either.

If you are ~~lucky~~ intentional, you can cultivate a group of trusted advisors who will tell you the truth, the whole truth, and nothing but the truth, rather than the angry truth-tellers listed above. I'm fortunate to have my spouse as one of my trusted advisors. She feels comfortable telling me, "I don't think that's a good idea," and much more. It's not always pleasant.

Our natural reaction is to explain ourselves. We've built up so many walls to prevent competing ideas from entering our echo chambers and cheerleader meetings, we don't give permission or space for people to call our baby ugly. Our defensiveness, rationalization, and justification are all built-in self-preservation responses that help us avoid emotional wounds. These coping strategies anoint our ego boo-boo with a healing balm, but in the long run, they cause weariness because relationships are damaged instead.

Have You Run That Past Your Helpmate?

When someone seeks my counsel on a decision, my first question is, "What does your spouse think?" If you can't have a conversation with your spouse, that's a red flag. Get counseling from someone you trust who is not in the same or worse situation than you are. I've learned the hard way how important it is to be in alignment with your spouse. In many ways, they know us better than we know ourselves.

Marriage is a partnership where two become one flesh, creating a sense of completeness. This oneness isn't just about unity but also about complementing each other and bringing balance to the relationship. My wife is detailed and sometimes grills me with questions like a good attorney would. It's lots of fun when she cross-examines me this way. Not!

I'm the opposite; I just want the big picture and may only remember 50% of what you tell me. I can't stand hearing how clocks are built, so just tell me the time. In day-to-day life, my lack of detail has led to many, how do I say, frustrating moments in our marriage. I might bring a business idea full of hope and joy to my wife, eager for her approval. Instead, she starts asking questions and raising doubts with her cross-examination. I'm thinking, *Where's the shared excitement? Don't you see the vision?*

It's amazing how often those details save us from mistakes. The process of defending my ideas sometimes drives me crazy, but I thank God for a wife I can depend on for wise counsel. Even though we may not agree 100%, we don't move forward unless there is unity. That's a policy I learned the hard way...

Your spouse, with all their honest and sometimes painful observations, might just be the secret agent the Lord has sent to shape you. They are there to grind down your rough edges and refine you. If they're getting on your last nerve, it might be time to ask what the Lord is trying to teach you through them.

In addition to my spouse, I have surrounded myself with many people who know me well and can speak into my life. The key is I don't keep secrets or live a double life. It takes a lot of energy to live two people's lives in one body, and it will wear you out.

Our spouses and trusted advisors have an advantage over us. They aren't emotionally attached to our firmly held beliefs and opinions. They can look at our situation or problem from an objective point of view, one with our best interests at heart. This ever-so-small separation between logic and emotion enables them to give us wise counsel.

It's the same reason we can offer others great advice on living their lives, raising their children, and managing their finances, yet we often turn around and do the opposite. Too often, I wish I had followed my own advice.

Invitation to Change My Mind

If you want people to give honest feedback, I suggest two steps. First, invite them. You can ask people about the "advantages and disadvantages" of an idea. These two words aren't emotionally loaded like "agree, disagree, good, or bad." The idea is to create a zero-entry (swimming) pool where people can start pushing back slowly and early. Don't wait until you're in the deep end to ask for feedback.

Second, resist the urge to argue. Friends and coworkers will shut down when they realize you don't actually want honest feedback. I still struggle with this at unexpected times, proving growth is a process.

Lastly, there is a special power you should pray God gives you. It's called **the ability to change your mind**. Oh, the horror. I think it's a special power because most people don't have it. I've noticed most people dig in and hold tight to their opinions. They become inflexible and defensive when challenged, refusing to consider opposing data.

We live in a hyperpolarized world where everyone wants to change other people's thinking without trying to understand their point of view. Admitting you might be wrong requires humility, which cuts through narcissism and ego. Getting alone in solitude and seeking the Lord helps us identify wrong motives and half-truths we might be believing.

Like driving a car, the further you look back, the more you can see where you were driving poorly. Have you ever looked back on your life five, ten, or twenty years later to review your mistakes in retrospect? Learning about our own biases and accepting we need to be able to change our minds when presented with better information is essential. Yet, most people will never admit they were wrong or change their minds. What good is a trusted advisor if they can never change your mind?

Sometimes Right, Always Certain

There are things I look back on from ten years ago that I believed, felt, and knew to be true, but later learned were not true.

Paul says, "Now, a person who is put in charge as a manager must be faithful. As for me, it matters very little how I might be evaluated by you or by any human authority. I don't even trust my own judgment on this point.

> My conscience is clear, but that doesn't prove I'm right.

The Lord himself will examine me and decide."[27] Paul believed his motives were pure, but he admitted, "I don't even trust myself on this."

I'm sorry, but despite your confidence, your motives and emotions aren't always pure. You're not always right; everything you believe isn't always correct, and everything you feel isn't always a fact.

Show Me

In moments of solitude, it's a great time to ask the Lord, "What are the beliefs I hold right now, and have held for a long time, that aren't true and are based on lies, half-truths, or 99% truths?" As we begin to fix our thinking, it will change our direction. We can change our minds by asking God these questions if we have humility. In addition, I use the Bible as a compass for my true north, and I've never found any downside to following its principles.

There is a saying, "Pride leads to disgrace, but with humility comes wisdom." Wisdom and growth come when we let go of our pride and allow ourselves to be teachable. These teachable opportunities can arise from the hands of trusted advisors who genuinely care for you or from unfriendly and angry "truth tellers." You have some choice in the matter, so choose wisely. The openness to change and growth sets great leaders apart from defensive, weary leaders. Great leaders are not afraid to change their minds when encountering new evidence or insights. They are constantly evolving, learning, and growing. As a result, instead of striving, they find *soul rest*.

CHAPTER 13

Twenty-Four Hours

I USED TO HATE THE fact that I had to sleep. I decided the best way to cheat time was to cheat sleep. In college, I needed over seven hours a day to feel human. One semester, I fell into a routine where I would sleep four hours at night and then take a two-hour nap between classes. It was a miserable rhythm of life with too much ebb and not enough flow.

A few years later, I read another article about taking twenty-minute naps, six times a day. By reducing your sleep from the recommended seven hours a day to just two hours, you can add fifteen years of wakefulness to your life—imagine the productivity. The article stated the body would adapt, allowing you to fall into a deep sleep faster and experience REM sleep more quickly. This experiment lasted less than a day. I was trying to outsmart God's natural design for my life.

Still later, I tried sleeping six hours during the week and then catching up on the weekend. This philosophy originated from Loverboy's hit song, "Working for the Weekend," and it seemed to work for a few years.

However, after listening to some podcasts by leading researchers, I realized proper sleep is crucial to our bodies. Additionally, I discovered an incredible principle embedded in the book of Genesis. God created everything in six days, and mankind was created on the sixth day. Then man and God rested on the seventh day. Only after rest did he go to work.

Here's the big idea:

> You work from rest, not to rest.

As I embraced the science and the natural rhythm of sabbatical, I gave up on these goofy ideas of rewiring the universe and started looking for hacks that would help me sleep seven hours a night.

> God gave us sleep and sabbatical rest as a gift. Stop fighting it and learn to embrace it.

Fair Is a Place You Go to Show Your Pig

There are a lot of things in life that aren't fair. Where we are born, whether we are book smart or people smart, how adept our parents were, our health, and so on. We learn about fairness early in life, probably around the age of two or three. You give three pieces of candy to one child and one piece to the other child, and they will say, "That's not fair." It seems to be built in from birth.

My dad wouldn't allow us to say, "That's not fair," and I was probably big on saying it. I grew up in a town of about 3,500 people, which meant we had the town fairgrounds where animals were paraded around, rides were set up, and carnival games were played. I've lost more money playing rigged carnival games. I'll never forget the three-disc game or the machine gun that shot BBs designed to clear all the black on a target. But I digress.

When I said, "That's not fair," Dad would say, "Fair is a place you go to show your pig," and in our case, it really was.

I remember being out of college for only a couple of years and being young in my profession. The check-signing plates for manual checks were kept under lock and key in my office and were rarely used, except once a year for the executive's bonuses. I got to see every executive's bonus check before they did.

At a young age, I learned to be happy for others and their successes rather than being angry or jealous. I thank my dad for a definition of fairness early in life that I would later pass on to my kids.

Planned the Rest

There is one ingredient I wish I had talked about more with my kids: the importance of time management and prioritizing intentional periods of rest. The problem is when my kids were little, I didn't understand the proper ebb and flow of my physical and spiritual life. I didn't know a sabbatical could be something I could do every day, week, or month. I always thought it had to be at least one year long.

You can't teach something you don't know, but I'm learning it's never too late to model new habits, even for my adult children.

The Ten Commandments rank failing to take a day of rest once a week right alongside murder and lying.[28] Wow. Harsh.

Thank God we live in an age of grace. The challenge with a sabbatical isn't hatred or honesty; it's stewarding our time and priorities to include God and rest.

Time Steward

Life's not fair, but time is. It's perfectly equal for everyone. There are all of these uncontrollables in our lives, but time is the one principle that is 100% equal for everyone. Everyone gets twenty-four hours a day. How you steward time can be life changing. How someone stewards their time might be why you think someone else's life isn't "fair."

When I left the workplace structure, I wanted to relax and was selfish in that regard. Everyone has a way of checking out and doing nothing, which is okay in moderation. Some people enjoy watching TV, reading social media posts, jogging for four hours, biking all day, or playing video games. Other ways are either more expensive or more harmful, such as alcohol, drugs, gambling, and pornography. There are many other examples, but even seemingly good activities like fitness, hobbies, or sports can be taken to an extreme and become harmful.

Even though we may be relaxing or checking out when we do these things, they aren't the same as intentional and purpose-ful rest, where you can journal your thoughts, enjoy solitude, and pray without interruption. Now you know better than I did, so I encourage you to prioritize sabbatical rest as part of time stewardship.

I realized the benefits of daily sabbaticals (times of quiet) early in life, but it took me a while to appreciate the benefits of restoration during a weekly sabbatical. It wasn't until I figured out we work *from* rest, not *to* rest, that I started taking a weekly sabbath more seriously. It took decades to begin considering the idea of a sixty-hour sabbatical versus a family vacation. Undoubtedly, both have their place, and only you know your family's capacity to do one or both.

However, my longer sixty-hour sabbaticals provided moments of solitude, breaks from adrenaline, and physical healing through fasting and cell autophagy. In addition, I gained spiritual insights through prayer and journaling that I couldn't achieve in shorter time frames.

At our house, the weekly sabbatical always included church attendance. The church is a great place to start because it allows us to encourage one another. However, it doesn't fully address the nuances of rest and recuperation, nor does it fulfill the personal relationship with God, which is our real source of *soul rest* and requires one-on-one time to cultivate.

This prompted me to conduct a time audit. I began to identify areas where I was a poor steward and where I could eliminate waste. I don't think life has to be all work, all play, or all sabbatical rest. In fact, I think it needs to be balanced, but most of us lose track of our balance, and the first thing to go is sleep, quiet time, and sabbatical rest.

When I started disciplining myself to manage my time, I discovered I could read through the Bible in a year if I made it a daily habit. I noticed many of my friends had written a book. I asked them how, and what I found is they prioritized it and disciplined themselves to write daily. Wow, that was challenging. *Note: I didn't do that.*

I asked people where they found the time to take care of a lake house, and they said it was a family cleanup for the first two weekends. I asked how they started their business, and they took one day a week off to work on it.

You may think your time isn't under your control, and as a result of the decisions you've made in the past, it may not be in the short run. However, I promise that over the long term, spanning ten or more years, it will be entirely under your control, and a well-managed calendar guided by the Word of God can significantly impact your destiny.

With more time, you can improve your health, make more money, fix up a house, repair a car, learn to work on your AC or plumbing, paint your home, play with your kids, and go on a date night more often.

Over the years and decades, your life will reflect how well you steward your time, as well as your priorities and habits. I think we'll all be held accountable for how we spend our twenty-four hours, so now, I'm more careful how I use them. One thing is sure: We won't be able to use the excuse "it wasn't fair."

Twenty-Four Is Enough

God must have felt like twenty-four hours were enough when used properly. If you disagree, you'll have to take it up with Him. God says, "Make the most of every opportunity in these evil days." That means being intentional with our hours.

> Taking a sabbatical rest demonstrates our time is within our control and we're choosing to give it back to ourselves, others, and God. It's a deliberate act of submitting to the natural ebb and flow of life, and stops the

shallow apologies of too busy, too tired, next time, oops, and sorry.

It might be hard to accept we don't all have the same opportunities at birth, and we can't change that. But the good news is God can open doors no man can close and close doors no man can open.

The more I've planned my life around **rest**, the more productive the **rest** of my life has been. The great thing about time stewardship is that it's not complicated, but that doesn't mean it's easy. We need to review our priorities so when little time thieves creep into our calendar, we're quick to weed them out.

Invite a third party, such as your spouse or trusted advisor, to help you see blind spots. If you struggle to say no, then say, "I need to think about your request." Often, people ask us out of convenience. The better you steward your time, the more time you'll have for purposeful pauses, *soul rest*, and sabbaticals.

CHAPTER 14

Money Is a Test

WHEN WE WERE FIRST MARRIED, we went to church with another couple we knew from out of town. Susan and I put a check in the offering plate, and our friends added some cash. I guess our friends had seen us writing the check or something, because at lunch, my buddy said, "Why are you giving that much money?" I had this nice answer: "Well, we believe God owns everything, but He loves us so much He lets us keep most of it." My friend said, "He must really love us because He lets us keep all of it." We still laugh about that. People have such diverse views of money.

Some of Susan's and my biggest money tiffs have been over buying another pair of shoes or buying another fantasy football team. Early on in my corporate career, Susan worked about eight weeks a year. I found out my paycheck was *our* money, and her paycheck was *her* money. That didn't seem fair. When taxes rolled around, they had only withheld 1% of her pay for income taxes. I said, "Sweetheart, we are not in the 1% tax bracket; they need to take out more money from your check." Do you think she changed her withholdings? I'll refer you back to the chapter on learning to lose. Money is a highly contentious topic that generates significant stress and friction. Add another person into the mix, and you'll never see everything exactly the same.

How do you view money? The answer to the question is likely a combination of how you were raised, your view of God as a provider, and your current reality. This guides how you prioritize your spending and probably comes with a lot of emotion attached to it.

When you feel a strong emotion about something, poke around and ask why. How would you describe your emotional tie to money? Hate it? Love it? Close friend? Faithful provider? Evil adversary? Party buddies? Absent parent? Controlling boss? Your heart's desire? A radio playing in your mind 24/7? Mr. Wonderful? Unfaithful lover?

How you describe your emotions and relationship with money reveals a great deal, as the world's system is structured so we exchange our time, talent, or product for green pieces of paper. What are you willing to trade for this magical green paper?

> Are you exchanging your integrity, peace, or *soul rest* for temporary things (versus eternal), or for what you love that can't love you back?

What does a healthy relationship with money look like? Here are some of my ideas. It includes living below my means and avoiding debt, so I'm not stressed about paying bills or repaying debt. I think it encompasses investing and giving, two concepts embodying the idea of delayed gratification. The list could go on. I certainly haven't been perfect, and my investment decisions are riddled with regret. I've discovered I tend to buy stocks at high prices and sell them at low prices, resulting in a loss. I'm super smart that way.

As I began considering taking a one-year sabbatical, a wrestling match ensued in my mind between faith and fear. God first reminded me that He was my provider, not the company paying my salary. It's one thing to say God is your provider; it's another thing to walk that path. As I prayed about taking a sabbatical, the Lord was saying, "It's there for the taking."

I felt sure there was a version of myself and new ministry opportunities that could only be reached by taking a sabbatical, and it required me to walk off the ledge into the unknown. This step of faith into the unknown was an enormous black chasm, and I couldn't see where I was going.

I call this the *faith test*, and I think it begs the question:

> Do I trust God to provide for me when I can't see the outcome?

The reciprocal of the faith test is the *stewardship test*, which I would describe as follows: **Can God trust me with His resources?** These two questions summarize the money tests and represent two sides of the same coin. Don't worry if you've failed the faith test or stewardship test in the past because God is a good God and provides many retakes.

The Faith Test

Let's look at an example of the faith test. In late 2019, my son opened a fitness studio with our help. This time, unlike my earlier venture, I sought wise counsel, God's peace, and took my time counting the costs and praying. In addition, I realized I was always just a few months from my next mini-sabbatical, so I started waiting to make big decisions until after a time of rest and solitude. I was living from sabbatical to sabbatical. Lastly, we dedicated the business to God and gave him ownership, and we became stewards.

Little did we know COVID was on the way, and fitness (good health?) was not considered essential. It was scary, but we had faith, so we just prayed, "God, your business got shut down. You might want to look into it." It may sound like I'm joking, but we were serious. He sustained us during that crisis, and today it has multiplied in size.

> The faith test is passed when you go to God before you even start and trust Him in the unknown parts.

In doing so, God will provide daily bread through your business, job, or in miraculous ways. If you don't give it to Him, the pressure can be soul-crushing as you strive to make ends meet and fall deeper and deeper into debt and depression, trying to do it alone. This feeling of loneliness and hopelessness is what leads to the feeling of being *soulspent*. You will experience *soul rest* almost instantly if you demonstrate trust in God by inviting Him into your financial affairs. Warning: don't be surprised if He wants to review your checking account and credit card statements when He shows up.

We are told to pray this way: "Give us this day, our daily bread."[29] God says you don't have to be a hoarder because I will meet your daily needs. King David said, "I've never seen the righteous forsaken nor their seed [children] begging for bread."[30]

> The truth is, no one wants daily bread.

They want years and years of bread stored up, so they and their progeny can eat for generations without trusting God. There is a balance that leads us away from the extremes, such as "the wise man provides an inheritance to his children's children, and the borrower is a slave to the lender,"[31] meaning there is nothing wrong with saving.

Faith for a Dollar

I remember a time in college when my financial situation was "tight." After paying for my room and board, I had just $35 a month in disposable income. My dad said, "Just budget your money. You have about $1 a day." Thanks, Dad. I was struggling with the math. I still laugh at this advice.

One sunny afternoon during my last semester, while sitting on campus with less than one hundred dollars in my checking account, a group of art students and their teacher approached me. They started sketching me for their drawing class. After a few minutes, the teacher asked if I'd be willing to model for their drawing class the following Tuesday night for thirty-five dollars. I thought there might be room to get her up to fifty dollars. It's fun to be drawn, and I wondered how I would be portrayed. Then I found out what the catch was. I'd have to pose nude.

I'm embarrassed to say how hard that decision was, because thirty-five dollars was my entire disposable income for a month. I could make "a lot of money" in a couple of hours. It was a tempting offer, but I said no. It's wild how much "a lot of money" is to different people and what they are willing to do or trade to get it.

I'm glad they didn't offer me $10,000 because those sketches might now be on eBay. At that point in my life, my integrity might have been for sale "for the right price." Once you understand the value of your integrity, it isn't for sale at any price.

I'm sure many readers have faced similar dilemmas—being asked to do something illegal, immoral, unethical, or illicit for financial gain. I've heard many stories from my fellow *sabbatical takers*, and it's clear from my own life and watching others ruin their lives: Trusting God for your needs is a faith test.

The Stewardship Test

Once you begin to trust God to do His part in providing daily bread, you've opened up the faith region of your heart that might have otherwise been asleep or atrophied. The next test is the stewardship test, which answers the question, "Can God trust us to be good stewards of our daily bread?"[32] Stewardship is the other side of the faith test.

There's no better way to know than by reviewing your historical spending and planning a budget. This helps you see if you are living within your means, avoiding consumer debt, giving generously, and ensuring your spending reflects your priorities.

> I believe giving generously is necessary to inoculate oneself against greed and is proof that one is passing the stewardship test.

Less Money, More Miracles

When I was living on thirty-five dollars a month, I was earning $350 a month. My room and board were $280 a month. Please note: My parents blessed me by paying that expense for my first four years, but a fifth year was viewed as poor planning on my part. They had a budget, and I was no longer a line item. Still, I gave thirty-five dollars a month to charity.

Then, the Lord showed me a loophole I'd never seen before.

I bought every book before Christmas break, read them, and then took them back the first week of classes for a full refund. I saved around $300 on books, which is conveniently about ten times what I'd been giving each month. I attended class more prepared and knowledgeable, which enabled me to earn an A in all but one class and pass all parts of the CPA exam on my first attempt at the end of the semester. Plus, my new employer gave me a bonus for passing.

My school scholarship also expired that year, and I didn't have the money for the second semester. I found out that two or three people would be staying at the dorms during Christmas break to support students who weren't going home. I applied for one of those positions and was selected. That job was just enough to pay for the next semester's tuition and fees. However, no food was provided for about four weeks. My sister stopped by and gave me twenty dollars and five microwave dinners. I went to the store and made twenty dollars go as far as I knew how. I bought five pounds of sugar (9,000 calories), Kool-Aid, Ramen Noodles, spaghetti noodles, and a couple of other things. I remember nothing required a stove. That Christmas, the other guy staffing the dorm with me lived in town and invited me to his house for his family dinner. I ate like a king and brought home leftovers.

God takes care of His children. I was poor, but my cholesterol was 118, I could run a five-minute mile, I had about 10% body fat, I never woke up in the middle of the night to pee, I always slept eight hours a night, and I had less than $2,500 in debt.

How would my life have been different if I cut charity from the budget? I don't know for sure, but how I stewarded thirty-five, I believe, created the track record to be put in charge of more.

When you start giving your hard-earned money to an organization that may or may not use it exactly as you like, but you do it for the Lord's sake, you will see your faith grow and your trust in God grow. It will give you the courage to take a year off from work during your peak earnings season to embark on a great adventure.

The bottom line is there are numerous opportunities to learn and improve, particularly in the area of finances. So, keep striving to find balance, and remember that giving is a crucial part of the journey. Don't fret if you've misused money or made choices you're not proud of because there will be retests.

As you consistently pass the faith and stewardship tests, you'll find you're less stressed about money, and you won't trade your *soul rest* in the marketplace for green paper.

CHAPTER 15

I'll Rest When I'm a Success

How do you define success? Proverbs says, "Don't wear yourself out trying to get rich. Be wise enough to know when to quit."[33] Are you getting worn out chasing a title at work, a certain bank balance, a specific car, or a house in the perfect neighborhood? Those pursuits won't be worth it if you become *soulspent*.

When I quit my job, I calculated I'd have "enough" to take a year off, but I was tempted to skip this sabbatical and continue working until full retirement age, so I'd have "more than enough." I lost a lot of stock because I quit before age 59½. It wasn't an easy decision, but I kept hearing this echo in my mind: *It's there for the taking. It's there for the taking.* Thankfully, I had trusted advisors praying with me about the decision. I had developed a life plan and tapped into the ebb and flow God had created.

As a result, it gave me the courage to walk away for a season, whereas some people can't help themselves. John Rockefeller was worth about $400 billion in inflation-adjusted dollars. Someone asked him, "How much is enough?" He said, "Just a little bit more."

When we reach an important goal or milestone in our success journey, it triggers the release of feel-good chemicals, such as dopamine and endorphins. With these chemicals working so hard in our bodies to make us happy, you aren't just chasing success and money; you are chasing the elusive high created by these chemicals. In the workplace, rewards and incentives, coupled with a bit of fear of loss, create a huge motivation to keep us pushing forward even when we are tired. How clever of life. Just don't forget life in this world eventually ends; therefore, don't let the urgent capture the eternal.

Personal Mission Statement

Success is elusive because it's hard to measure and highly personal. I suggest defining your life purpose or personal mission statement, then establishing goals for each pillar beneath it, such as health, family, business, spirituality, community, finances, and leisure. The book *Living Forward* by Michael Hyatt and Daniel Harkavy is an excellent guide to help you do this. I spent one of my early mini-sabbaticals going through this book and writing my life plan.

I've met people who have served prison sentences and are full of joy, while those who live in big houses are depressed. I think that's because some people have it all on the outside but are dead on the inside. The zombie apocalypse may be real, but it may be those who are *soulspent* going through life numb.

As you begin to consider your life as multidimensional and set goals in all areas, including spiritually connecting with God and allowing for rest and renewal, your goals might change.

Just as I added sabbaticals later in life, I started having a desire to operate in the entrepreneurial sphere.

I realized, despite my great job, I couldn't hand it over to my kids when I was gone, and there wasn't room to operate in all my giftings as an employee. However, if I became a business owner under God's authority, I'd have greater flexibility; it could be a family adventure, and my kids would have it after I was gone. This realization led me to change my business pillar to include entrepreneurship.

Where do these desires to own a business, write a song, design a machine, or other ideas come from? David said, "Delight yourself in the Lord and He will give you the desires of your heart."[34] The Lord is the one who puts those desires there when you delight in Him. Follow the formula of delighting in God first, and you'll stay away from other motivations, such as greed, envy, and jealousy.

My last day at work was Friday, January 5. I had nothing planned for the next twelve months except to visit family and friends and travel. But that following Monday, January 8, something came over me. I was inspired to start two companies. I jumped on the computer and, in just a few hours, registered two LLCs. I purchased the domain name www.sabbaticaltaker.com and officially registered it as an LLC on the first Monday after I retired.

I felt many people in Corporate America could benefit from discovering *soul rest*. I was thinking about writing a book, creating a website where people could connect, and recording some related podcasts. The website www.sabbaticaltaker.com and the publication of this book made that dream happen. I would have had so much regret if I had never pursued my dream.

The other LLC I formed that day was 3.14 Catalyst. The name is based on Pi, chemical reactions, Exodus 3:14 "I AM sent me," and Proverbs 3:14 "wisdom greater than gold." I loved coming up with the name and registering the domain.

My first business venture for 3.14 Catalyst involved minting silver coins. I wanted to buy silver but couldn't find coins that resonated with me. I wanted them to be faith based, so I contacted a mint, bought silver, created artwork, and had some manufactured. I can't tell you how much joy, dopamine, and serotonin I felt as I held that coin.

Pursuing a dream is fun and a good addition to your pillars, but run your dreams past wise counsel. Do not take your financial vehicle of life and crash it into the wall, chasing high-risk ventures that require leverage and promise returns too good to be true. Include the counsel of many, give your spouse veto power, talk with a financial advisor, get legal advice early, and check with a banker before making a significant investment that might require a cash flow loan.

Think Small and Pivot

Instead of spending a big chunk of savings or taking a loan to open a restaurant, think about an idea that is small and cheap but, when multiplied, becomes worth a lot. For example, buy one ATM, one vending machine, or one lawn mower, and when it pays for itself, buy another. Listen to the Lord, and be ready to pivot. If the brook dries up and the ravens stop bringing food (i.e., sales), that might be God's way of saying "move along."[35]

The Lord works in peculiar ways. Here are four people who took unusual routes to fulfill their purpose in life:

- Vera Wang started as a figure skater and then transitioned to a magazine editor. After being passed over for a promotion, she launched her luxury wedding dress line.
- George Shinn writes about finishing near the bottom of his high school class, but he excelled in the workplace and eventually bought an NBA team.
- Ray Bradbury couldn't afford to go to college, so he spent his time in libraries, self-educating. He sold papers on the corner and wrote short stories. At the age of thirty-three, he wrote a book in just nine days in the basement of the UCLA library using a coin-operated typewriter. The book was *Fahrenheit 451,* which went on to sell ten million copies.
- Craig Groeschel graduated from college with a degree in marketing and worked for a Fortune 500 company. At the age of twenty-eight, he decided to start a church in his garage with his wife and a few others. Today, his church has over 74,000 attendees on any given Sunday across twelve states. They also created a Bible app that has been downloaded one billion times and is available in over 3,300 versions and 2,100 languages.

From pastor to designer, and everything in between, be encouraged: God can color outside the lines. You can't put God in a box because He can make a way where there seems to be no way.[36] He can partner with you on a path that may not make sense when viewed from the outside. You have a life purpose bigger than success as defined by money or accomplishments. Your chosen path and goals may seem unusual or insignificant to others. That's okay. Go in faith and be **your** version of awesome.

Plan Ahead

Preparing your purpose statement in advance is wise and guards against becoming *soulspent*. We are all addicted to these reward chemicals: dopamine, serotonin, and endorphins. The excitement of the moment and adrenaline can make us say "yes" when our purpose statement tells us "no." In his book *Seven Habits of Highly Effective People,* Stephen R. Covey says it this way: "Begin with the end in mind."

What's my life purpose statement? "As I delight in the Lord, I will courageously pursue the purposes and dreams God laid out for me, with family and friends, on a journey that leaves me feeling rested because I intentionally pause to connect with God and others." I have goals for each of the areas mentioned above, but they all align with this one overarching idea.

What's your definition? I encourage you to write it down and run it past your family and friends to see if they have any additional insights to share. Reevaluate your definition of success so it's not one-dimensional and invites God into the process. Then, map out some intentional pauses along the journey. When we think about "success" this way, we don't become *soulspent;* instead, we experience *soul rest* and find joy in the journey.

CHAPTER 16

Take a Penny, Leave a Quarter

I HOPE YOU ARE READING this book with another person, or even better, in a group. Living life in a community of like-minded people is so meaningful and fulfilling. When I go on one of my three mini-sabbaticals each year with others, we gather around a campfire to share what we hope to gain from the experience. It's primarily rest and solitude, but a problem or goal may also be on your mind.

Steve went on a sabbatical with us. I could never understand his business. He finally explained he was in the fire-retardant business for marine equipment. He achieved success by purchasing a product and working with a third party to improve it. He was able to secure a patent and identify a sales niche. When successful people explain how they got from A to Z, it's like seeing The Great Oz behind the curtain. Their success can often be applied to other industries, whether they give feedback directly to me or to another person in the group. It's an incredible opportunity to apply success principles from one industry to my industry. Sometimes, the best part of my sabbatical is the solitude, as I feel God is speaking directly to me; at other times, it's the evening brainstorming and sharing around the campfire, as God speaks through others.

My friend Tim has a great story from his mini-sabbaticals. Tim has a lawn care business and has been doing well for many years. His company had found an equilibrium based on his ability to sell and service his customers, balanced by his ability to hire and retain good staff. He was busy every day and tied to the area during lawn season, from about February to November in the South. This is the story of many business owners. Then, Chris joined our sabbaticals. Chris had a massive lawn service, plus another three or four other businesses, sixty miles away. Chris shared how he staffed his company, and three years later, Tim traveled to Europe twice during the spring and summer, making more money than ever before. He learned from Chris and solved his hiring shortfall, which had always been his bottleneck.

Through small groups, I met someone who had been to prison. His business fell into financial distress, and instead of facing possible bankruptcy, he tried to keep it alive with creative financing. If he had gotten godly counsel and a lawyer, he might have declared bankruptcy or worked it out with the bank. Instead, he spent part of his life incarcerated in an attempt to fix his problem alone. Could this describe you? Are you cash-poor and responsibility-overloaded? Open your life up to wise counsel so you don't go down with the ship. Invite God to give you *soul rest* so you can move forward.

Part of elevating your career or life is finding people to bounce ideas off of and to mentor or coach you. The right person can guide your career, marriage, parenting, business start-up, or any other area, as you benefit from the voice of experience. The exact same concept applies to the person who feels *soulspent* and believes no one else would understand or has struggled with similar issues. Opening yourself up to others can be like piercing a blister. Tears might flow, but it will be the beginning of your healing.

On my mini-sabbaticals, I share my problem or goal with a small group of trusted advisors and write about it in my journal. There's a great saying, "Write the vision and engrave it so plainly upon tablets that everyone who passes may be able to read it easily and quickly as he hastens by."[37] Our problem statement or goals are more likely to be solved or met when shared with someone who can help or hold us accountable. Not surprisingly, a study supports the power of writing and sharing goals (Matthews and Bouchard, 2015).

We are designed to need other people. There's a better version of ourselves that can only be found with the help of other people. God designed us for relationships, and when we circumvent that design, we fall prey to our weaknesses and biases. The struggle to include others in our journey is often due to pride or shame. I encourage you to do it, even if you're afraid.

A proverb says plans go wrong for a lack of (wise) advice; many advisers bring success, or it could be said there is wisdom in the counsel of many.[38] You may carry a burden into your group that someone else can lift away. It's sort of like the old "take a penny, leave a penny" philosophy, but it's better.

Choose Between a Blessing and a Curse

God has granted us free will, and it should be a bit frightening. You can grow, thrive, and become more than you ever hoped or imagined. You can go places, see things, and live a life you only dreamed of. You also have the God-given freedom to destroy your life, become addicted, make regretful comments, act hastily, and take unnecessary or unwise risks.

Ignoring *soul rest* warning signs and the Feedback Loop of Life is easy when alone because confirmation bias will cause you to seek comfort only in those who agree with you. You are choosing between a future filled with joy or one filled with regrets when you decide to include others on the journey rather than go alone. Choose life.

Right Place, Right Time

Many times, when I see people destroy their lives, it's because they were in the wrong place at the wrong time. King David decided to stay home, "when kings go out to battle." He woke up from a nap and saw a beautiful woman bathing. He requested her presence at the palace. They had an escapade, and she ended up pregnant. When David found out, he requested her husband return from the battlefield. Uriah was one of his most loyal servants and a good friend. David had dinner with him, got him drunk, and sent him home to have sex with his wife. Uriah was a stand-up guy and wouldn't enjoy himself while everyone else was at war.

What did David do? David sent Uriah back to the front lines with a letter asking his commander to make sure the enemy killed Uriah, plus make it look like an accident. A horrible story of sex, drugs (alcohol), lying, cover-up, and murder. How did it all start? Wrong place, wrong time. Talk about how one thing leads to another.[39]

I worked with a nurse who told me most gunshot victims, when asked what happened, said, "I was minding my own business." I guess selling illegal drugs at 1:00 a.m. on the street corner is technically minding *the* business. We used "minding my own business" as a joke around the office. It's code for "**I was in the wrong place at the wrong time, but I don't want to take responsibility.**"

My dad spent a summer custom-cutting wheat from Oklahoma to the Canadian border. The days were long, and the only breaks were due to rainouts. During a rainout in the Dakotas, he met a couple of hooligans at the local blacksmith shop. They were going on a fun trip to the Black Hills and invited him. Due to a desire to save money and character, he declined the offer, and it's a good thing he did. Those two gentlemen went on a little robbery spree that landed them in prison. Dad avoided it all by staying focused and avoiding the offer to be in the wrong place at the wrong time.

You are in the right place at the right time when you take an intentional pause or meet with a group of like-minded *sabbatical takers*. Did you get a competing offer? Go out of town with the guys to the football game? Drink too much, so your bad behavior is excused or forgotten? Hmmm. Wrong place, wrong time. One of those groups of friends will hold you accountable, and you will instinctively want to do better. If you have a 1% desire to do more and be more, or a 1% fear of ruining your life, consider joining a group meeting with other *sabbatical takers*. Don't delay. Just do it.

Please Leave Your Bags

Wisdom That Leads to Soul Rest is designed to provide rest, restore you, prevent you from wearing out so quickly, and guide you toward *soul rest*. Reading this book with someone else, participating in small-group meetings, and taking mini-sabbaticals are all designed by God to lighten your load while helping you carry someone else's. The difference is their load won't come with the same emotional baggage you just dropped off with them.

> I call it "take a penny, leave a quarter" because you go home with a smaller burden than you came with.

Small groups, trusted advisors, and like-minded *sabbatical takers* help alleviate the feeling of being overwhelmed and reinvigorate you as you realize you're not alone. The truth is, you're not the only one facing challenges, so don't get sucked into a vortex of fatigue and isolation. Your sabbatical-minded friends will refresh you, helping you find joy in your journey. What a great addition to *soul rest*.

CHAPTER 17

The Compounding Nature of God

IF YOU'VE EVER BEEN AROUND farming or ranching, you understand the compounding nature of God. My brother-in-law bought three cows and a bull. Five years later, nature took its course, and his herd had grown to forty. When you plant wheat, you put about ninety pounds of wheat into the ground per acre, and you hope to harvest over 4,000 pounds per acre. Time with the Lord leads to compounding results, and His math can impact our faith, finances, relationships, health, or any other area we give to Him. The great thing is, God doesn't need a lot to work with, but He does require at least a seed of faith, a penny of investment, or a single prayer.

God describes His math and His compounding nature this way: "Those who receive God's Word and take it to heart are like good soil—they bear fruit and produce a harvest, some a hundredfold, some sixty, and some thirty."[40] This begs the question, "How much is a hundredfold?"

Origami

I love math and statistics, so follow along with this experiment. Take a piece of paper and fold it in half. Fold it in half a second time. Fold it in half a third time. Fold it in half a fourth time. Now, count how many "squares" you have after folding it four times. If you counted and folded correctly, you have 16 squares after four folds: 1, 2, 4, 8, 16. At first, it appears to be addition (1+1=2) or multiplication, but God's growth is continuous multiplication. God says His kingdom is a hundredfold, so how many squares would that be? 1,267,650,600 followed by twenty-one more zeros! That's a little over one nonillion, and our imaginary piece of paper would extend to the universe's outer reaches as it becomes many trillions of miles thick after being folded over and over.

Another example of exponential growth comes from a two-inch domino. The momentum from one domino can knock over a larger three-inch domino, which can knock over a larger domino that is 4½ inches tall. Guess how many dominoes it takes to reach the moon, which is 238,000 miles away? It's the fifty-eighth domino. That's the power of compound growth.

God can do amazing miracles when you give Him something to work with. He needs something small, tiny, or thin that you put in His hands. Once you put it in His hands, resist the urge to take it back, possibly just to worry over it. During a lifetime, He will make it something remarkable. That's how God's math works. It is not subtraction, which takes away, or division that separates us and makes us smaller, and it's even better than addition or multiplication because, over time, it becomes exponential.

Facade Fading, Interior Glowing

If you are sixty years old and just beginning to offer something small to God, don't worry—He can do miracles. No, you may not feel twenty-five again, but He can certainly multiply your spiritual nature. You might know someone who is sixty years old who has claimed to have faith for forty years, yet they are mean, greedy, and unloving. You can start your faith journey at any age and pass them in six months when you invest time and live authentically. Don't let age discourage you.

Our physical bodies eventually fade away. I wish a bell had sounded and a voice had said, "This is the last time you will run a 5:00-minute mile." Or, "This is the last time you will pass your driver's exam without glasses." It's a sad reality as you age that you won't run quite as fast, jump as high, see as clearly, or hear as well. In addition, your sense of pain will become a little duller, so shots don't hurt as much, and your twentieth vacation isn't quite as exciting as your first.

Our physical bodies are like flowers, blooming and then, over time, wilting. Conveniently, I was in full bloom when I got married. As our physical being withers, our spiritual side grows stronger in wisdom and experiences a deeper connection with God, **if we so desire**. As our body slowly moves from this life to the next, our hunger and thirst for what's eternal and spiritual naturally grows. It's been said this way, "Therefore, we do not lose heart, but though our outer person is decaying, yet our inner person is being renewed day by day. For our momentary, light affliction is producing for us an eternal weight of glory far beyond all comparison."

Your spirit man is growing and has only the limits you set. Your spirit can't grow when you continue to put up walls of doubt and refuse to access the faith area of your heart. Your spirit has a hundredfold potential, but you control the accelerator and the brake.

> So, press the gas, because the more your spiritual man grows, the more you will find *soul rest*.

The psalmist says:
> "But the godly will flourish like palm trees and grow strong like the cedars of Lebanon.
> For they are transplanted to the Lord's own house.
> They flourish in the courts of our God.
> Even in old age, they will still produce fruit; they will remain vital and green.
> They will declare, 'The Lord is just! He is my rock! There is no evil in him!'"[41]

There is no retirement in the Kingdom of God. He will always have work for you. He continues to bring people into your life who need the voice of experience or words of encouragement. Even Daniel was over eighty years old when he was thrown into the lion's den and was an advisor to the king. He still had significant assignments well past his "prime."

How to Journal

Another way to push the gas pedal is to journal your questions, allowing you to appreciate your journey and the insights it provides. You may not get the answer right away, but you'll be surprised how much you'll learn by journaling. Here are examples of questions I ask:

- Should I start _____? Should I stop _____?
- Am I spending my time and money appropriately?
- Should I spend more time with this person? Should I spend less time with that person?
- What do I need to eliminate from my life? What do I need to add to my life?
- Or something specific: Should I send 1,000 or 2,000 direct mail pieces?

Successful people are curious, so ask questions and don't claim to have all the answers. Writing forces us to word our questions clearly and succinctly. God encourages us to be inquisitive, saying, "Ask me, and I will tell you remarkable secrets you do not know about things to come."[42] God wants to share his secrets, but it's up to us to ask.

The wisdom book of Job asks, "Who gives intuition to the heart and instinct to the mind?"[43] It reminds us that God has endowed us with two inherent skills—instinct and intuition—and that it's our job to develop and hone them.

As your spiritual man grows, ensure you feed it a proper diet. Be mindful of what you let in through your eye and ear gates. There are tried-and-true books that yield kindness, patience, faith, love, and other good fruit we all want in our old age, but the Bible has been foundational to my growth. Only due to my selfishness or hypocrisy has it not "worked" for me. Additionally, surround yourself with people of good character who uplift and challenge you to be better.

If you're starting late, don't worry—start now. Give God your finances, your desires, your plans, your family, your job, your faith, and everything in between. When you submit and say, "Not my will, but Your will be done," you open up your life to the power of God's math.[44] He won't let you down.

CHAPTER 18

A Healthy Body

IN COLLEGE, I RAN TRACK and did a little bit of boxing. I was in six matches over two years and earned second place twice, as well as a broken rib, a hernia, headaches, a permanent neck tweak, plus I don't know what else. I saw a neurologist one day and was genuinely concerned about how I had used my head as a battering ram in football and boxing in my youth. I said, "I boxed in college. Could that increase my chances of Alzheimer's?" He wouldn't answer the question. All he would say was, "It's not good." I'm laughing about it now while I still have my wits, but it really isn't funny.

Boxing "suddenly" changed my health, but then family responsibilities and career goals became my "gradually." Gradual declines in your fitness or constant sleep deprivation over many decades will erode your energy and impact your mental, emotional, and spiritual life. You can't constantly overdraft your physical health and expect never to have to pay it back; you'll also owe compound interest. If you are feeling *soulspent*, I doubt physical exhaustion alone is the cause, but it provides fertile soil for other problems.

As I've gotten older, I've come to realize the value of prioritizing my health. I don't take it for granted like I used to—I no longer choose to use my head as a battering ram. There's nothing like a concussion, bruise, or broken bone to make you a little wiser.

Healthy Hacks

I'm not going to try to cover physical fitness from A to Z. Science is constantly evolving, and we are always learning. I suggest reading or listening to Gary Brecka, for example. He provides free information backed by science. This is just one person doing great work in the field of health and fitness, and there are many more. Additionally, ensure you have a local healthcare professional who can tailor your care and conduct a comprehensive physical examination.

Some of the big ideas in fitness that helped me:
- Resistance training over cardio training
- Walking over running
- Eating single-ingredient foods over junk foods, fried foods, or unsustainable diets
- Getting seven or more hours of sleep with the help of supplements, mattresses, and nightly sleep rituals, such as no screen time one hour before bed
- Behavioral systems, such as food prep and clothing prep, instead of relying on motivation
- Sunny days and dark nights
- The power of fasting

I've adopted as many of these healthy hacks as possible into my life, but I want to share more about fasting. A longer sixty-hour fast is one habit I rarely see practiced and few people talk about. It's a habit that can be transformative, leading to increased energy, reduced brain fog, and freedom from sickness and disease. This practice goes back thousands of years to Traditional Chinese Medicine (TCM) and biblical writings. Plus, it's **free**.

Fasting

During my mini-sabbaticals, I do a sixty-hour fast and only drink water and coffee, but my coffee asks for cream, so I'm not a purist. The goal is to do a longer fast three times a year. You can do it more often or less often, but let me give you a reason for doing it three times a year. After thirty-six hours, your body enters autophagy, a process where healthy white blood cells remove unhealthy cells, allowing your body to heal and self-cleanse. In addition, your red blood cells are replaced approximately every 120 days, so you are stress-testing your body to ensure the weak are removed and the strong survive.

The idea of fasting isn't just about food. Fasting affects the incredibly complex, yet hidden, world of hormones and enzymes, and is a restorative process. The surprising benefit of fasting is that your metabolism and energy increase when you fast for sixty hours (Fernández-Verdejo, Mey, and Ravussin 2023). As you discipline your physical body, your spiritual senses suddenly engage, making your times of solitude, prayer, and journaling all the more powerful. That's why the Bible says, "when you fast."[45] Plus, as you try to give up anything physical for three days, you discover what controls you. Whether it's nicotine, caffeine, sugar, food, sex, TV, or cell phones, fasting shows us the things that own us; we don't own them. It's time to regain control.

Fasting has been shown to have many health benefits, which scientists did not expect or predict. These benefits include improvements for individuals with cancer, enhanced cell regeneration, a healthier gut microbiome, improved mental clarity and memory, and better regulation of insulin levels. At the end of the chapter are a few studies that highlight the benefits of fasting longer than forty-eight hours.

If you can't complete sixty hours, start with a smaller goal and gradually extend the length each time you fast. Why isn't fasting discussed more often? My research shows over $100 billion a year is spent on drug studies. I thank God for the discoveries of modern medicine, and I'm not saying zero dollars have been spent on finding the benefits of fasting. However, there's little financial motivation for studies showing a sixty-hour fast could be as effective as, or outperform, drug ABCDE.

In addition to the studies cited below, there is the wisdom of ancient Chinese medicine, which teaches fasting benefits three common ailments: digestive health, detoxification, and mental clarity. I included these study references at the end of the book.

That's why when I take a mini-sabbatical, I also fast. I discipline my physical body so I can get off the adrenaline highs, disconnect from stress, and physically rest while I spiritually grow. There are benefits to this purposeful pause science hasn't fully explained and isn't financially motivated to decipher. Yet, the resulting *soul rest* is undeniable.

Feeling physically strong and healthy has numerous benefits and is closely related to your mental and spiritual health. Fasting is one of the top things I do to increase my creativity, improve my performance, lose weight, start new habits, and break old ones. I don't ever want to stop fasting because I believe it can be foundational in both improving performance and restoring the soul-weary traveler. Join me in adding this practice to your life, if you are able.

If you can't fast from food, find something else meaningful to fast from. You might want to consider giving up your digital media for a few hours, days, or longer. I've been on-call for so many years that I'm as addicted to my phone as anyone. I put screentime limits on some of my favorite apps, but I'm guilty of blowing through those stop signs. Find that thing that owns you instead of you owning it, and give it up for a period of time. When you do it in connection with solitude, prayer, and other spiritual disciplines, you'll experience physical and spiritual benefits to your soul.

In summary, don't dismiss the idea of fasting. Let this be one of the hard disciplines you choose for the benefit of your long-term health. While you are abstaining from food or something else important, you will be taking back control of your life, breaking free from addictions, and opening yourself up spiritually to receive what God has in store for you. One thing I'm certain He intends for you is *soul rest*.

A quick word of caution. I'm not a doctor, and I don't know your personal health history. Most people can safely fast, but if you're on certain medications, taking supplements, or have a medical condition, it's wise to talk with your healthcare provider first.

CHAPTER 19:

Worship[46]

WHEN MOST PEOPLE THINK OF worship, they think about listening to music, but I often prefer silence. That's because worship is more than just songs; it's a spiritual experience. The dictionary defines it as **ascribing worth** to something of value, and throughout the Bible, it means to **bow down**.

God invites us and allows us to be in His presence when we worship. It's really remarkable if you think about it. The more you are in His presence, the more you will intimately know and experience God. He's a loving God who gives grace when it isn't deserved and shows mercy to those who deserve judgment. He forgives the unforgivable and takes the time to talk to the "unimportant" people in the world. He sees the potential in people.

He is holy and without sin. The more I'm in His presence through worship, the more I begin to reflect and become like Him. Of course, becoming more loving and holy is a process.

We were created to worship, and the proof is we will find or create something to worship. Sometimes we worship and attribute worth to physical things such as cars, money, drugs, or any other golden calves that consume our time and money.

There is literally an idol for everything under the sun—including the sun!

These idols generally give us moments of euphoria, but instead of bringing long-term satisfaction, that euphoria fades, leaving us empty. If you're addicted to porn, you can never see enough pictures to be satisfied. If you are greedy, you will never be content with what you already have. Our idols steal time, money, and attention from the most vulnerable areas of our lives—such as sleep, prayer, worship, and charity—because they demand more and more in pursuit of new highs and bigger stimuli.

However, the human body is designed for refractory periods, and greater stimulation often leads to greater emptiness. These idols can't satisfy, and instead, they slowly ensnare our every thought and motive. Worshiping God sets us free from these vicious, unfulfilling cycles and leads to victory!

To bow down is a physical act that shows reverence to something greater than ourselves, but God says true worshipers do so in spirit and truth, meaning that what is really happening is a heart issue. That's why worship taps into the hidden faith region of the soul and rejuvenates your spirit, much like gratitude is beneficial for mental well-being. As your spirit is restored, your mind is renewed, and your heart posture changes. You will begin to root out the enemy's lies and reject your idol's demands for more of you, resulting in *soul rest*.

Searching for Lies

During my one-year sabbatical, God revealed some lies and half-truths from long, long ago. I started waking up almost every night between 2:00 a.m. and 3:00 a.m. for about thirty days. I figured if God was waking me up, He wants me to pray, and if the devil is behind it, he will stop doing it when he sees I use it as an opportunity to pray.

Therefore, I got up each night for about thirty days to pray, find promises I could stand on, give God glory for who He is (worship), and listen from the heart while in His presence. I finally got an electric blanket for my prayer chair, making it more appealing during chilly nights.

I enjoyed the peace and solitude during these nights and sought God for some specific situations. Shockingly, I was getting less sleep, but I wasn't tired at all. It might have been diet, exercise, supplements, or God. I don't know. But the more I was in His presence through worship, the more I began to see the onion of my life peeled down to more profound truths.

I started thinking about actions and attitudes I had as a youth and young adult. I exhibited rebellion, took shortcuts, avoided putting in the effort, used inappropriate language, took the forgiveness-over-permission route, and acted selfishly, among other bad habits. In various ways, I realized even as an adult, some of those old habits had made their way into my thoughts or actions.

The lies and half-truths I believed, as well as my lazy or sinful patterns, were little foxes spoiling my harvest in life. God revealed these thoughts and peeled the onion of my life slowly and carefully, layer by layer. This happened because I was taking the time to worship and pray. It took almost a year-long sabbatical before I started seeing some thought patterns and behaviors in a more critical light.

You may need help from a third party, or you may simply need to spend more time in God's presence.

This part of worship is a little scary. We don't really want to critically examine our lives, change our minds, or admit that some of our beliefs or feelings could be wrong because we can all be arrogant and unyielding. That's why we need to worship: it's humbling and will make peeling the onion as painless as possible.

I Can See Clearer

It takes faith to find spiritual rest because you have to believe (or want to believe) you are worshiping a God who is bigger than you, created you for a purpose, loves you, wants the best for you, and will be there both through the good and bad times.

We've touched on some of these presumptions in prior chapters, but you can't ascribe worth to God if you don't believe these truths about Him. I partnered with God and asked Him to reveal His heart. I challenge you to do the same thing.

Sounds Scary

Worship might sound scary if you are ashamed of your past, too embarrassed by what other people think, too busy to take the time, afraid to be vulnerable, or simply don't think you know how.

These are all sneaky lies the enemy slips in to keep you from enjoying an intimate relationship with God. You might not feel like you are worthy to worship, but His Word says He will be there. God inhabits the praises of His people. Worship will change you from the inside out, providing a layer of insulation from the cold realities of life as your mind and desires change.

There's a Creator

I hope you aren't struggling with the idea that God exists. It's hard to ascribe value to something you think is all made up. Some people are wrestling with the science or logic of God, thereby building walls that separate them from God and prevent them from operating in the realm of faith. I'm not going to spend a lot of time trying to convince you, but the following few paragraphs are for you.

Trigger Warning: You could become emotional when you read the following sentence.

The faith required to believe in evolution is greater than the faith needed to believe in God, and yes, both require faith.

I understand evolution might have made sense when hypothesized in the 1800s, before we understood bacteria, viruses, DNA, RNA, electricity, computers, cell phones, TVs, amino acids, cars, planes, etc. Darwin questioned his own theory, saying, "This Abstract, which I now publish, must necessarily be imperfect" (Darwin 1859, Introduction).

The idea of "evolution" happening such that a male and female evolve at the same time and same place so they can safely grow up, find food, water, clothing, shelter, and reproduce lots of healthy offspring all within a nice little circle of time and space takes a lot of faith. Therefore, I choose to put my faith in a Creator who designed the Earth to be inhabitable.

The creation is perfectly balanced. The Earth is tilted at 23½ degrees, resulting in seasons that prevent overheating or prolonged freezing. Earth's atmosphere is approximately 21% oxygen, which is beneficial because concentrations below 12% or above 30% would be fatal to human life. It's located about

150 million miles from the sun, which is convenient because being 20% closer or farther would lead to extinction.

Plants use carbon dioxide and release oxygen; without this symbiotic relationship, humans would die in approximately 150 years. Water expands and floats when it freezes instead of contracting and sinking, which is lucky because we would all be gone in less than 200 years if water contracted like virtually every other compound. It's almost as if all this "luck" is by design.

You may struggle with faith because you've spent your life understanding and explaining the universe using science, but **some concepts must be experienced.** These are the come-and-see moments in life. Even if science can explain 95% of cell life, plant life, space, time, oceans, and human emotions, it still can't explain 100%. There is the unknown. Could God exist in the 5% you know nothing about?

> Believing in a creator gives us purpose, which means we are here by design. We are here because someone loves us and has a plan for us.

That should bring us peace. Plus, it doesn't take any more faith than believing it's all by accident. King David says, "You made all the delicate inner parts of my body and knit me together in my mother's womb. Thank you for making me so wonderfully complex. Your workmanship is marvelous—how well I know it."

When we struggle to bow down to God from our hearts and give Him the glory, our souls become weary. That's because internally we are wrestling with Him, whether we know it or not.

The patriarch Jacob was in a wrestling match with God. It says by morning, he was weary and went away limping. Our physical strength is limited.

As we worship God and spend time in His presence, we will naturally want to be like Him. For me, that means I am becoming more loving and authentic. Then I surround myself with others who give God the glory, and we cheer each other on. What you find is the longer you live this way, the more authentic you are, and the less soul weary you will be.

You might be physically or mentally fatigued, but your spirit will be at peace. You can stop running from faith and fighting with God. Suddenly, you will realize you have found a new level of *soul rest*.

CHAPTER 20

Repentance[47]

A SABBATICAL LIFESTYLE CAN BE lived every day, and *soul rest* can be experienced continuously. However, our peace can be disrupted when our relationships aren't whole. Sometimes we have to apologize to a friend, a co-worker, or God Himself. Admitting errors and apologizing are crucial ingredients in any healthy relationship. A shallow "sorry I got caught" doesn't cut it.

Repentance takes apologizing to the next level and includes searching our heart and motives. God will bring to your mind times when you didn't live out the Golden Rule by loving others as much as you love yourself. In addition, there are those times we don't love God with all our heart, mind, soul, and strength. We may know what we need to apologize for without asking, or He may remind us of situations that weren't top of mind.

Repentance is a time to reflect with humility and genuinely express remorse. Of course, the best way to express remorse is not to do it again. But regardless of our imperfections, God provides forgiveness to all who humbly repent. The story of the prodigal son highlights His love and mercy.

Two Prodigals?

A man had two sons, and one of them asked for his half of the inheritance. It's a bold, arrogant request. Imagine liquidating your assets so one child could have their share to do what they want with it before you die. He was kind of saying, "I wish you were dead." This arrogant son then leaves the family farm, meeting all the usual suspects—users who snuggle up to you when times are good and when you have money to share. Eventually, the money disappears, and so do these types of "friends."

As long as he had food, friends, clothing, and shelter, he didn't need his Father. He was numb to his spiritual needs. It wasn't until he had a time of solitude and fasting (wait, isn't that a mini-sabbatical?) thrust on him by his circumstances that he started doing some soul-searching. It was during the hard times of loneliness, abandonment, hunger, bankruptcy, and humiliation he came to his senses. He decided to go home, apologize from the heart (i.e., repent), and ask if he could return as a hired hand.

When he was still far off, the Father saw him coming. He was keeping an eye out for him. The Father let him repent, but cut him off mid-sentence, telling him he was still a son and to bring a family robe and prepare a feast.

This shows God is not an earthly father who wants to rub it in, ask where the money went, make you suffer, hand you a bill, and give you a timeline for returning as a son. He's a good God who removes our sins as far as the east is from the west. It's easier to repent when you realize God is a good and loving Father who is the ultimate provider of *soul rest*.

One definition of prodigal is "spending money freely and recklessly." You can see why the story is often called the Prodigal Son, although the term is never used in the story. The son was wasteful with his money. The interesting thing is a second definition of prodigal is "having or giving something on a lavish scale." I guess you could say God is prodigal in how He lavishly heaps grace and forgiveness on us. What great peace and comfort.

Dealing with the past will lighten your load and allow you to enjoy the relationships and experiences of the present. If you keep going back to the past, you may not have dealt with it in a healthy way.

> True repentance comes from conviction and should be a healthy experience that leaves you feeling clean, not dirty and depressed, because repentance is not motivated by condemnation. Instead, it's the kindness of God that leads to repentance.

Yes, we have memories, and they can't be erased. If you are stuck in the past, unable to move forward, or find it difficult to enjoy the present, you may need the help of a third party, such as a friend, counselor, physician, or other professional.

We all need to take responsibility for our decisions and maybe even take back the part we put on someone else by saying, "No, I was 10% responsible, so it wouldn't have happened without me. Therefore, I will take 100% responsibility." Healthy relationships require us to apologize and admit we've had a hand in hurting others.

Plow It Up

God's Spirit connects with our spirit and provides a gentle con-
viction or whisper that reminds us of what we need to repent
from. If we ignore that inner whisper, it will eventually fade
away, but in the process of turning a deaf ear to the Spirit, you
will harden your heart. That's why we are advised to plow up
the fallow ground of our heart.

Less than 200 years ago, most people were farmers, so
everyone was familiar with a plow, but you may not be. Sometimes, a farm might have been uncared for, ignored, overgrazed,
or rutted. In this situation, the master farmer may decide the
soil needs a one-time reset.

First, he will plow this stubborn and firm ground. The plow
digs down deep, turning the soil over so that the hidden, com-
pacted dirt below can be exposed to the sun. However, the plow
leaves large chunks of dirt that need to be dealt with further.
Next, he takes a disc that breaks these large chunks into small
pieces. It is only after the work of the plow and the disc that
the soil can be planted.

When God says to plow up our fallow ground, He is making a point.

> You can't expect a bountiful harvest from rock-hard
> soil. It needs to be exposed to the Son.

When we plow up the fallow ground of our heart, we are
doing a one-time reset. This comes after a season of numbness,
allowing the hidden parts of us to come to the surface, where
they can be broken down with God's love and planted with

seeds of righteousness. Keeping the land clean is easier once it's had a reset.

Talk It Out

When you write down your ideas, you may start to see patterns emerge as you reflect on your life. Introspection is one of the most important ways leaders grow and the *soulspent* heal. Often, I pray silently inside my head, but there is a case for praying out loud or writing them down, thus shining a light on them.

Extra sleep and proper sleep routines can help improve your physical well-being, but repentance is a spiritual exercise that addresses our relationship with the Creator and the faith aspect of the heart.

Believe it or not, your soul is crying out for this time of cleansing. I can't prove it. You just have to taste and see for yourself. When you start repenting, you'll know how refreshing and renewing it is. God is good and will provide a healing balm of forgiveness, and if needed, we should also forgive ourselves.

I once heard the formula described as "admit it, quit it, and forget it." If any of these three steps are challenging, don't hesitate to ask for help.

> Most people can't break habits and addictions on their own.

You can't get unstuck by yourself because your mind is powerful at manipulating you to get what it wants, such as a dopamine hit.

Stop the ride and get off if you're caught in a negative feedback loop from habits and addictions. You may need someone outside the ride to hit the stop button, support you, and hold you accountable for not getting back on.

Are you having an emotional response to this chapter? It's likely because an old wound or hurt was touched, a festering splinter trying to reach the surface. Stop, drop, and roll—don't wait for the perfect moment to spend time repenting and receiving forgiveness. Do it now. A good soul wash is critical in restoring soul health at the soul level. You'll be surprised how much lighter your load is when repentance and forgiveness remove the heaviness of life.

CHAPTER 21

To Obey Is Better Than Sacrifice

I STARTED TAKING MINI-SABBATICALS IN 2014 and moved out of state in 2018. To take my mini-sabbatical with my friends after 2018, I needed to fly, rent a car, and take two days of vacation, while others who lived in town had a fraction of the costs. Since others were paying so much less, I knew God was patting me on the back for my sacrifice (joking).

Shame(?) on Me

During our mini-sabbaticals, in addition to fasting and solitude, we spent a few hours each night sharing ideas and challenging each other in small groups while enjoying the light of a campfire. During the campfire, David said, "The most important thing from sabbatical isn't the sacrifice we all make to be here...It's obeying what we are told when we go home." That hit me like a ton of bricks.

A few years earlier, I had written in my journal, "Write a note to Mom and Dad thanking them." I should have done it right away, but somehow, I found something else to do. *No worries, I can always do it later,* I thought. Sadly, life got busy, and later never came. Honestly, I totally forgot about it. Shame(?) on me.

I spoke with my mom in early March 2020, and Mom and Dad had just completed a ten-day driving trip across America to visit my son, aunt, sister, and nieces, and then return home. It was about 1,200 miles of driving, and Dad felt horrible. He swore that was the last driving trip he would ever take.

On March 14, 2020, I received the call that Dad had fallen during the night. He'd been pretty sick with a cold and was trying to go to the bathroom. He was a young eighty-two-year-old living at home, checking on farm ground, and playing in real estate. He could stand to lose weight, but those living in glass houses shouldn't throw stones. When I heard he had fallen, I decided to run home to check on him.

I was working at a hospital at the time, and we had maybe two or three confirmed cases of COVID, but for almost a dozen more cases, we were waiting five days or more to receive lab results. At the time, all COVID tests were sent to the state, and with my parents living in a town of less than 4,000, it seemed like an unlikely diagnosis.

I arrived home Friday night, and Dad looked a lot sicker than I anticipated. In your mind, your parents are perpetually young, but on this day, Dad looked old and frail. I asked him some questions to check his mental acuity: "Do you know what today is?" He couldn't answer, so Mom piped up, "He knows it's Friday." I asked, "When is your birthday?" He was a bit confused, so Mom stepped in with the correct date. All I could conclude was Mom's mental acuity was excellent, and Dad's was suspect. In retrospect, I realize he was oxygen deprived.

He started taking some medications that were later semi-banned. In his case, it seemed to make a difference. The next morning, he was clear-minded, laughing, and back to his old self. He was doing so well, I decided to return to the hospital, where we were on call over the weekend, to plan for an expected patient surge as the world shut down.

Unfortunately, twenty-four hours later, Dad was hospitalized, and we weren't allowed to visit him. Shortly after admission, he was intubated so we couldn't speak to him nor he to us, and you can guess how the story ends. He died on April 1, 2020, and only ten people were allowed at the funeral.

I was told, based on my county of residence, I couldn't attend unless I could quarantine for two weeks. This left me with sorrow and regret for not following through on my intention to write him a letter during my sabbatical.

You may have your version of this story or something else, leaving you looking backward with regret. The good news is God's blessings are new every morning.[48] We don't have to live in the past. This story reminds me to take action.

> Do the next right thing as soon as possible.[49]

This is the key to obedience. Therefore, I want to encourage you to do what you already know you should do. God appreciates your sacrifice of time, finances, and talents for others. All you're giving is impacting lives, and you shouldn't stop. But don't be confused; obedience is greater than sacrifice.[50] Don't live with the regret of delay or, even worse, disobedience. The end goal isn't sacrifice but the transformation that comes from living a life of obedience and humility.[51] As the fire crackled,

I realized a true sabbatical isn't just about quiet time, intentional pauses, worship, repentance, solitude, prayer, journaling, and sacrifice, but importantly, includes the obedience and changed life we take home.

When I think about my dad, I reflect on what I wish I had said and done. Instead of dwelling on the past, I choose to learn from it. I choose to do better in the future. I don't accept the "shame" my past mistakes want to attach to me. No. I reject "shame on me." Instead, I declare, request, and believe "blessings on me."

You might be thinking, "Bret, this is incredibly sad." Don't get me wrong. I'm ticked at the situation and my lack of obedience. However, as a hospital CEO, I was able to empathize with others and lead the charge to change the rule of "no visitors." I believe I will be reunited with my Dad, and it will be all joy with no tears.[52]

The Narrowing Road

The one thing I'm certain of is that I've not arrived. I purposely prioritize *soul rest* to avoid becoming *soulspent*, but it's a journey. In life, there is a wide, easy-to-follow road. This is the road that leads to heartbreak and hell.

Then there is the narrow road[53] filled with love, forgiveness of others, repentance, worship, gratitude, losing on purpose, preferring and serving others, obedience, etc. I've learned through thirty mini-sabbaticals, a sabbatical lifestyle, and a year-long sabbatical that the narrow road gets narrower.

There were thoughts and behaviors from when I was a teenager that the Lord started dealing with me about, and I couldn't do them when I was thirty. Then, in my forties, I had to give up the habits I thought were okay in my thirties. Now, at fifty-eight years old, I have observed patterns from my childhood that I still need to change.

I have learned the rhythm of *soul rest* through purposeful pauses I can't ignore. I can't go back to "working for the weekend" so I can rest, nor do I want to! Once I tasted and experienced the benefit of the rested life and the rested soul, there's no going back.

My education in *soul rest* comes after decades of doing it the hard way. I've shared the life lessons I learned, hoping to lighten your load. You can take your knowledge and experience, combined with mine, and go even further. The more you know, the more is expected of you.[54]

After reading this book, the road will be forever narrower, but that's okay because God is saving you from pain and regret. God wants you to pass on your tips and tricks for finding rest to someone looking for something a nap or a vacation can't fix. Show them the way, even if they see what a failure you've been in learning it yourself.

CHAPTER 22

I'm Ready for Mini-Sabbatical

MY FIRST MINI-SABBATICAL WAS ALONG the Red River in Mississippi. My friend Gary and I heard someone teach on this verse: "Three times each year, every man in Israel must appear before the Sovereign, the LORD."[55]

Don't worry, ladies, this includes you. We found two little cabins along the river with air conditioning and rented them for Sunday and Monday nights. It was about a two-hour drive, and along the way, Gary said, "I think we should fast." I was a little surprised and thought, *Really? It's a good thing my wife didn't pack me a survival snack pack.*

We pulled up to these two cabins in the woods, and there were two guys a little younger than us waiting for us. I didn't know if this was how life ended or if these were the owners. It turned out they were the owners, and these cabins were brand new. They were curious about what two adult men would do in the woods for two days. We didn't joke about doing anything nefarious, and we provided the craziest cover story in the world if we were up to no good. We were here to fast and pray.

It was about 4:00 p.m. on Sunday, and we settled into our cabins. I later learned Gary was taking detailed notes (journaling) and would have a record of every mini-sabbatical we had ever taken. I, on the other hand, carried on with my lazy strategy of taking no notes because I thought, *I'll remember this later. It's too important to forget.* I used this strategy my sophomore year in high school, the day before a biology test, and it got me kicked out of class.

Teacher: "Bret, are you going to take notes?"
Bret: "Um...I don't think so."
Teacher: "Leave...Get out of here...Now."

I'm what's known as a late developer, so there's still hope for you or your child.

That night, around 7:00 p.m., we got together to sit around a campfire and talked for two or three hours. We talked about everything: our families, struggles, dreams, businesses, insights, failures, and everything else. We prayed with and for each other. It was a powerful time. It was dark, and when you are away from the rest of the world out in the woods, you naturally get sleepy around nightfall. As noted earlier, I hate the dark and was not crazy about being in the woods in a cabin by myself, so I checked the closets, behind the shower curtains, under the bed, locked the door, and tucked myself into bed.

The next day was Monday, and somehow we instinctively knew to give the other person solitude; without stating it as a policy, we took a vow of silence. During the day, I napped like a worn-out pup, took long walks, read my Bible, journaled, and practiced the habits of worship and repentance. I even enjoyed listening to worship music.

That night, we got together for another campfire moment. We shared what we had been thinking and doing. After I realized Gary was taking notes, I decided I should too. The fire was mesmerizing, and the conversation was flowing with only short moments of silence. A few hours later it was time to go back to the scary cabin. The second night, I didn't sleep as well. I had taken so many naps I wasn't tired, and I was hungry. I spent my time awake doing some journaling, but eventually I did fall asleep.

Suddenly, it was 7:00 a.m. and we were ready to drive back home. We broke our fast together with a hearty breakfast, which, by the way, is not the recommended way to break a fast. Thankfully, nature did not create a crisis. I arrived back home and was ready to go back to the office by 10:30 a.m. Mini-sabbatical number one was complete, and it was amazing. It was more than I had hoped or expected as I experienced a new level of *soul rest*.

We went back to our small group and told them how awesome it was, suggesting they should try it. In the meantime, we went on six more mini-sabbaticals, except for missing a couple due to unexpected crises, which is okay. You can turn a good thing into something so rigid it replaces the heart behind it, which in this case is the intentional time of solitude and rest to connect with the Creator.

Sabbatical Embers Spread

Fast forward to sabbatical number seven, and Gary had scheduled everything so anyone in our small group could come. I hate to say it, but I never really cared if the group grew. I was enjoying my party of two, but he had a bigger vision. At first, it became just four or five people, which I found surprisingly awesome as well as I gained insights from new *sabbatical takers*. Then, he opened it up even further, and we eventually had to rent a campground with forty-two cabins. As a result, we started meeting around 5:00 p.m. to explain the program to the new people and then broke out into multiple campfires, each with a small, intimate group.

Over one hundred people have come to one or more mini-sabbaticals. It has been a powerful way to introduce the natural ebb and flow to an increasing number of people. It would have never happened if one person hadn't had the vision and discipline to arrange it for everyone. Gary's leadership reduced the activation energy for those who wanted to go but didn't want to plan it. Maybe you are the planner in your group and can take the lead in planning a mini-sabbatical.

No two sabbaticals are the same. I have visited seven different campsites. Sometimes fasting is easy, and other times it can be difficult. During one sabbatical, I may average twelve hours of sleep a day, and during another, I only sleep seven hours. There is variation in the campfire talks, in repentance, in worship, and in how much you journal. A couple of times, we changed it up and had food on Monday night, which shortened the fast but increased the fellowship. Sometimes people have to leave at 4:00 a.m. on Tuesday before they can say goodbye. It's a sad reminder of how hard it is to give up sixty hours.

It's All Mapped Out

Susan and I did a sabbatical in Kansas, staying in a camper on farmland I will someday inherit and had been to many times before. We discussed my taking a year-long sabbatical, which, as you now know, I did. Then, while we were exploring the 160 acres, we found something I'd never seen before. It was a survey marker from the U.S. Bureau of Reclamation placed there in 1961 when the land was being mapped. It was at the highest point for miles around and absolutely gorgeous. That night, I wrote in my journal, "I think God is saying, '**Trust Me. You are the map I platted and on the road I planned**.'"

The next day, we drove around a bit on dirt roads to explore this semi-remote area. We came upon a stone marker showing the trail Zebulon Pike, an American explorer, took in 1806. There was another map on the marker. Another confirmation.

It's so awesome to look back and read this now, knowing it led me to a year-long sabbatical, plus a book, plus...I don't know what else. That's why it's a faith journey with sabbatical rest stops along the way.

CHAPTER 23

See You on Sabbatical

WE ARE COMING TO THE end, my friend. I would love it if you went on a mini-sabbatical. I know how much *soul rest* it will provide you and how beneficial it will be. I would love to go with you! The reality is, I can't be everywhere at once—and the beauty is you don't need me. I'm adding resources on how to do a mini-sabbatical yourself at my website: www.sabbaticaltaker.com.

There is another sabbatical that I saved for the end. It's the heavenly rest that Hebrews 4 talks about.[56] It lasts a really long time—eternity. It's promised to everyone who wants to enter by faith.[57] I might not meet you in this life, but I hope and pray I meet you in our forever home. If you are not sure you'll be there, I provide more information at www.sabbaticaltaker.com to make sure you are!

For the driven, I hope I've shown you how to go further without becoming *soulspent*. For those who are feeling drained, I hope I've shown you where your energy is leaking. For both of you, I hope you become lifelong *sabbatical takers*.

I am a Sabbatical Taker™.

Acknowledgments

"To the Lord God who provided the wisdom and inspiration.

"Look, God is all-powerful. Who is a teacher like him?"
(Job 36:22, NLT)

To my wife, Susan, who provided feedback on every chapter, helped me maintain my tone, and showed endless patience while I sat in my chair writing and rewriting.

To my daughter, Kayley, who always offered a fresh and unique point of view and helped with the book cover.

To my son, Alec, who competently managed our business so I could focus on this project.

To my sisters, Venette and Denise, whose feedback near the end helped me finish strong.

To Gary, my *sabbatical taker* partner–thank you for walking this journey beside me.

To Alec, Ryan, Ryan, and Scott–the first group to go through the book chapter by chapter for twenty weeks as a small group study when it was still raw. Your honesty helped keep the message strong and centered.

To Kim, who kept me focused with steady, insightful feedback.

To Alison, who provided as much editing as I'd let her, so I could still be *colloquial, cliché, trite,* and a little *hickish.*

To my fellow *sabbatical takers,* with whom I've shared so many campfire chats, who inspired me and built my faith.

And to those who read early drafts and encouraged me that this was an important message worth sharing–thank you.

References

Research summaries in this book are paraphrased from published scientific studies. The interpretations are the author's and are not endorsed by the original researchers.

Chapter 8: The Faith Journey of Parenting

Yao, Grace, Jin-Shei Lai, Sofia F. Garcia, Susan Yount, and David Cella. 2023. "Positive and Negative Psychosocial Impacts on Cancer Survivors." *Scientific Reports* 13 (14749). This study found that cancer survivors experience both positive growth and negative challenges in psychosocial well-being after treatment.

National Institutes of Health. 2021. "The Power of Peers: Who Influences Your Health?" *NIH News in Health*, September 2021. U.S. Department of Health and Human Services. This article highlighted how peer influence can significantly shape health behaviors and outcomes.

Chapter 9: Gratitude

Kahneman, Daniel. "Attention and Effort." *Englewood Cliffs*, NJ: Prentice-Hall, 1973. This research explains how attention is a limited mental resource and that our brains selectively focus on what seems most important, filtering out the rest.

Begg, Ian, Donald Maxwell, John O. Mitterer, and Grant Harris. 1986. "Estimates of Frequency: Attribute or Attribution?" *Journal of Experimental Psychology: Learning, Memory, and Cognition* 12 (4): 496–508. This study shows that people's judgments of how often something occurs depend less on actual repetition and more on how distinctive or memorable it feels.

Clear, James. *Atomic Habits: An Easy & Proven Way to Build Good Habits & Break Bad Ones.* New York: Avery, 2018. This book popularizes the idea that small shifts in focus and daily behavior compound over time, using examples like the "red car theory" to illustrate how attention shapes perception.

"Gratitude Journaling and Parental Well-Being." *Springer*, 2022. This study showed that parents who practiced gratitude journaling reported higher well-being and lower stress levels.

"Gratitude Practice Enhancing Psychological Well-Being." *The Positive Psychology People*, 2017. This article explained how consistent gratitude practice enhances psychological well-being and builds resilience.

"Gratitude and Positive Memory Bias." *Current Psychology* (Springer), 2018. This research found that gratitude strengthens a positive memory bias, helping individuals recall uplifting experiences more readily than negative ones.

Chapter 11: Good Decisions

Mullainathan, S., et al. 2023. "Scarcity and Cognitive Function: Implications for Stress Responses." *Journal of Economic Psychology* 94: 102574. https://doi.org/10.1016/j.joep.2022.102574. This study found that scarcity consumes mental bandwidth, reducing cognitive function and amplifying stress responses.

Griskevicius, V., et al. 2022. "The Influence of Resource Scarcity on Behavioral and Physiological Stress Responses." *Psychological Science* 33 (9): 1456–68. https://doi.org/10.1177/09567976221079123. This research showed that perceived resource scarcity heightens stress physiology and shifts behavior toward short-term survival strategies.

Huijsmans, I., et al. 2024. "Scarcity Mindset and Its Neurobiological Effects: A Review." *Neuroscience & Biobehavioral Reviews* 158: 105543. https://doi.org/10.1016/j.neubiorev.2023.105543. This review summarizes how a scarcity mindset alters brain function, influencing decision-making, stress regulation, and long-term well-being.

Tricking Our Brains into Fight or Flight Mode

Kothgassner, O. D., et al. 2023. "Virtual Reality and Stress Response: Physiological Reactions to Imagined Threats." *Frontiers in Psychology* 14: 1051234. https://doi.org/10.3389/fpsyg.2023.1051234. This study demonstrated that virtual reality can elicit real physiological stress responses, showing that imagined threats activate the body similarly to real ones.

McEwen, B. S., et al. 2022. "The Brain on Stress: Neurobiological Underpinnings of Imagined and Real Stressors." *Neuroscience & Biobehavioral Reviews* 141: 104829. https://doi.org/10.1016/j.neubiorev.2022.104829. This review highlighted how the brain processes both imagined and real stressors, with overlapping pathways that influence long-term health outcomes.

Yaribeygi, H., et al. 2024. "The Impact of Mental Stress on Physiological Systems." *Stress* 27 (1): 15–23. https://doi.org/10.1080/10253890.2023.2291745. This article outlined how chronic mental stress disrupts multiple physiological systems, including cardiovascular, endocrine, and immune function.

Worry Yourself Sick

Brosschot, J. F., et al. 2023. "Perseverative Cognition and Health: The Role of Prolonged Stress-Related Thinking." *Health Psychology Review*. https://doi.org/10.1080/17437199.2023.2176643. This review found that prolonged stress-related thinking, such as worry and rumination, has significant negative effects on both mental and physical health.

Clancy, F., et al. 2022. "Worry and Health: A Prospective Study on the Physical Health Consequences of Anxiety." *Journal of Anxiety Disorders* 89: 102576. https://doi.org/10.1016/j.janxdis.2022.102576. This prospective study showed that chronic worry and anxiety predict poorer physical health outcomes over time.

Tully, P. J., et al. 2024. "Anxiety, Worry, and Cardiovascular Health: A Systematic Review." *Psychosomatic Medicine* 86 (3): 189–97. https://doi.org/10.1097/PSY.0000000000001289. This systematic review concluded that anxiety and worry are strongly associated with increased cardiovascular risk and adverse heart health outcomes.

Chapter 17: The Compounding Nature of God

Matthews, J., and C. Bouchard. 2015. "The Effect of Writing Goals on Goal Achievement: A Study at Dominican University of California." Dominican University of California. This study found that individuals who wrote down their goals, shared them with others, and maintained accountability were significantly more likely to achieve them.

Chapter 18: A Healthy Body

Afzal, M., et al. 2023. "Multifaceted Benefits of Walking for Healthy Aging: From Blue Zones to Molecular Mechanisms." *Geroscience* 45 (6): 3041–56. This study found walking supports longevity and healthy aging by improving cardiovascular, metabolic, and cellular processes, as seen in populations living in Blue Zones.

Paluch, A. E., et al. 2024. "Resistance Exercise Training in Individuals with and without Cardiovascular Disease: 2023 Update." *Circulation* 149 (3): e217–31. This study found resistance training improves strength, metabolic health, and survival in both healthy individuals and those with cardiovascular disease.

Cheung, J., et al. 2022. "Effect of a Whole-Food Plant-Based Diet on Postprandial Sleepiness: A Pilot Study." *Journal of Clinical Sleep Medicine* 18 (2): 589–97. This study found a whole-food plant-based diet reduces post-meal drowsiness, suggesting diet quality directly influences daytime energy and alertness.

Siengsukon, C. F., et al. 2017. "Sleep Health Promotion: Practical Information for Physical Therapists." *Physical Therapy* 97 (8): 805–12. This study found promoting healthy sleep through behavioral and lifestyle strategies enhances physical therapy outcomes and overall well-being.

Burke, L. E., et al. 2022. "Effect of a Mobile Health-Enhanced Behavior Change Intervention on Weight Loss in Adults: The SMART Randomized Clinical Trial." *Obesity* (Silver Spring) 30 (7): 1378–88. This study found using structured digital health tools combined with behavioral coaching significantly improves long-term weight loss results.

Seven Studies Highlighting the Benefits of Prolonged Fasting

Cheng, S., et al. 2021. "Impact of Prolonged Fasting on Gut Microbiome and Immunity." *Journal of Clinical Investigation* 131 (14): e146377. This study found that prolonged fasting reshapes the gut microbiome and strengthens immune function.

Safdie, F., et al. 2020. "Prolonged Fasting Protects Normal Cells but Not Cancer Cells against Chemotherapy." *Cell Stem Cell* 26 (5): 682–96. This study showed that prolonged fasting protects normal cells but leaves cancer cells vulnerable to chemotherapy.

Wei, M., et al. 2021. "Prolonged Fasting Enhances Insulin Sensitivity and Alters Metabolic Biomarkers." *Diabetes Care* 44 (8): 1899–906. This study demonstrated that prolonged fasting enhances insulin sensitivity and improves key metabolic biomarkers.

Mattson, M. P., et al. 2020. "Fasting and Brain Function: From Molecules to Man." *Nature Reviews Neuroscience* 21 (12): 757–73. This study reported that fasting supports brain health by improving cognitive function and protecting neurons.

Anton, R. F., et al. 2021. "Prolonged Fasting and Addiction: A Neurobiological Perspective." *Journal of Addiction Medicine* 15 (6): 447–55. This study revealed that prolonged fasting influences brain pathways related to addiction, suggesting therapeutic potential.

Longo, V. D., et al. 2020. "Fasting and Enzyme Regulation: A Key to Health and Longevity." *Cell Metabolism* 31 (3): 456–71. This study concluded that fasting regulates enzymes in ways that promote health and longevity.

De Cabo, R., and M. P. Mattson. 2020. "Effects of Intermittent Fasting on Health, Aging, and Disease." *New England Journal of Medicine* 381 (26): 2541–51. This review found that intermittent fasting benefits overall health, slows aging, and reduces disease risk.

Traditional Chinese Medicine

Chang, A. 2021. "Fasting in Traditional Chinese Medicine." *Journal of Integrative Medicine* 19 (3): 210–16. This study explained how fasting is used in Traditional Chinese Medicine to balance energy and promote healing.

Li, H. 2020. "The Role of Fasting in Detoxification: A TCM Perspective." *Chinese Medical Journal* (Engl) 133 (22): 2673–78. This study described how fasting supports detoxification processes within Traditional Chinese Medicine.

Wang, Y. 2021. "Mental Clarity through Fasting: Insights from Traditional Chinese Medicine." *Asian Journal of Traditional Medicines* 16 (1): 34–41. This study reported that fasting is linked to improved mental clarity and focus in Traditional Chinese Medicine.

Additional Studies Including Intermittent Fasting Benefits

Fernández-Verdejo, Rodrigo, John T. Mey, and Eric Ravussin. 2023. "Effects of Ketone Bodies on Energy Expenditure, Substrate Utilization, and Energy Intake in Humans." *Journal of Nutritional Biochemistry*. This study showed that ketone bodies influence how the body burns energy, shifts fuel use, and regulates appetite in humans.

Mattson, M. P., et al. 2017. "Impact of Intermittent Fasting on Health and Disease Processes." *Cell Metabolism* 26 (2): 265–80. This study reviewed evidence that intermittent fasting improves metabolic health and reduces risks for multiple chronic diseases.

Cheng, C. W., et al. 2017. "Prolonged Fasting Reduces IGF-1/PKA to Promote Hematopoietic-Stem-Cell-Based Regeneration and Reverse Immunosuppression." *Cell Stem Cell* 20 (6): 766–80. This study found that prolonged fasting lowers IGF-1/PKA signaling, which regenerates blood stem cells and boosts immune function.

Lee, C., et al. 2016. "Fasting-Mimicking Diet and Markers/Risk Factors for Aging, Diabetes, Cancer, and Cardiovascular Disease." *Nature Communications* 7: 10101. This study reported that a fasting-mimicking diet improved markers of aging, metabolism, and disease risk in humans.

Chapter 20

Darwin, Charles. 1859. *On the Origin of Species by Means of Natural Selection*. London: John Murray. (Quoted from the "Introduction.")

About the Author

BRET KOLMAN VENTURED ON A one-year sabbatical after twenty-one years as a hospital CEO and eight years as a CFO, delivering top-tier quality and engagement by leading from a rested soul.

He holds degrees in Accounting, Finance, and a Master's in Healthcare Administration.

Today, Bret serves his community through the Chamber of Commerce, a local foundation, and his church—still a lifelong sabbatical taker and Bible student.

He and Susan have two adult children (Kayley, Alec), a daughter-in-love (Madeline), and one grandbaby they adore.

Bret once took remedial English (pass/fail)—so writing this book feels like a God-sized miracle.

Connect or book him to speak: www.sabbaticaltaker.com

Endnotes

1   Romans 12:18

2   Luke 6:38

3   Genesis 3:6

4   Acts 26:14

5   Exodus 20:1-17

6   Ephesians 6:1

7   Luke 22:42

8   James 4:6

9   Mark 4:24 (NLT)

10 Paraphrased from John 3:16 and John 8:11

11 Matthew 5:45

12 Paraphrased from Jeremiah 29:11 and 1 Peter 5:7 (NLT)

13 Judges 6:36–40; 7:1–8

14 James 1:2 (AMP)

15 Daniel 10:2-13

16 Galations 6:9 (AMP)

17 Philippians 4:8 (NLT)

18 John 16:33; 1 Thessalonians 5:18 (NLT)

19 Zephaniah 3:17 (NLT)

20 Psalm 139:17–18 (NLT)

21 1 John 4:18 (NLT)

22 Luke 6:12–16

23 Proverbs 15:22

24 James 1:5

25 Luke 10:5–6

26 Romans 14:17

27 1 Corinthians 4:2–4 (NLT)

28 Exodus 20:8–11

29 Matthew 6:11

30 Psalm 37:25

31 Proverbs 13:22; 22:7

32 Luke 16:10–11

33 Proverbs 23:4

34 Psalm 37:4

35 1 Kings 17:2–7

36 Isaiah 43:16–19

37 Habakkuk 2:2 (AMP)

38 Proverbs 15:22, paraphrase

39 2 Samuel 11:1–17

40 Matthew 13:23, paraphrase

41 Psalm 92:12–15 (NLT)

42 Jeremiah 33:3 (NLT)

43 Job 38:36 (NLT)

44 Luke 22:42, paraphrase

45 Matthew 6:16–18

46 This chapter draws on multiple passages from Scripture, including but not limited to:
John 4:23–24; Psalm 95:6; Psalm 100:4; Ephesians 2:8–9; Titus 3:5; Luke 19:10; John 4:7–26; 1 Peter 1:16; 2 Corinthians 3:18; Isaiah 43:7; Exodus 32:4; Ecclesiastes 1:9; Jeremiah 2:13; Ecclesiastes 5:10; Matthew 6:24; Psalm 115:8; John 8:36; Philippians 2:10–11; Romans 12:2; John 8:44; Song of Solomon 2:15; Psalm 139:23–24; Proverbs 11:14; Lamentations 3:40; Hebrews 11:6; Jeremiah 29:11; Psalm 22:3; Genesis 1:1; Psalm 139:13–14; Genesis 32:24–31; Matthew 11:28–29.

47 This chapter draws on multiple passages from Scripture, including but not limited to:
Matthew 5:23–24; 2 Corinthians 7:10; Matthew 7:12; Mark 12:30; Luke 15:11–24; 1 John 1:9; Psalm 103:12; Matthew 11:28–29; Ephesians 1:7–8; Romans 2:4; Hebrews 3:15; Hosea 10:12; John 3:20–21; James 5:16; Psalm 51:10,17; Psalm 34:8; Jeremiah 8:22; Philippians 3:13; Galatians 6:1–2.

48 Lamentations 3:22–23

49 James 4:17, paraphrased

50 1 Samuel 15:22, paraphrased

51 Romans 12:1–2, paraphrased

52 Revelation 21:4, paraphrased

53 Matthew 7:13–14, paraphrased

54 Luke 12:48, paraphrased

55 Exodus 23:17

56 Hebrews 4:9–11, paraphrased

57 Ephesians 2:8–9, paraphrased

www.ingramcontent.com/pod-product-compliance
Lightning Source LLC
Chambersburg PA
CBHW071745120626
46550CB00002B/674